The Divine Feminine

Virginia Ramey Mollenkott

THE DIVINE FEMININE

*The Biblical Imagery
of God as Female*

CROSSROAD · NEW YORK

1983
The Crossroad Publishing Company
575 Lexington Avenue, New York, NY 10022

Library of Congress Cataloging in Publication Data

Mollenkott, Virginia R.
The divine feminine.

Bibliography: p.
1. Femininity of God—Biblical teaching.   I. Title.
BS544.M64   1983   220.6′4   82-23542
ISBN 0-8245-0565-4

For
Debra Lynn Morrison,
who enables me to find my tears
and therefore my laughter

Contents

·1·

The Problem

In a recent Peanuts cartoon, Snoopy sits in front of the typewriter atop his doghouse laboring over an article to be entitled "Beauty Tips." Triumphantly he produces sentence one: "Always remember that beauty is only skin deep." But something feels wrong about that. After an inner search for relevance, he changes the final words to "fur deep."

The next day, however, he is visited by Woodstock, the diminutive chicken. After Snoopy has proudly shared his opener that "beauty is only fur deep," Woodstock gives him some strong advice in chicken language. As a result, Snoopy changes his conclusion to "feather deep."

Because he is trying to communicate inclusively with animals of many sorts, Snoopy is up against a very serious problem. Fortunately, the problem is eased considerably for those of us who are writing for a human audience. The only potentially exclusive distinctive that shows up in English grammar is the gender distinction of male, female, or neuter. With relatively little effort, grammar can be manipulated so that females as well as males are included and affirmed.

It seems natural to assume that Christian people, eager to transmit the Good News that the Creator loves each human being equally and unconditionally, would be right in the vanguard of those who utilize inclusive language. Yet a visit to almost any church on Sunday morning indicates that alas, it is not happening that way. Whereas a "secular" publisher like McGraw–Hill has insisted on inclusive language for almost a decade, the language of Christian preaching, prayer, and hymnody is still laden with exclusive-sounding references to men, man, brothers, sons, and the God of Abraham, Isaac, and Jacob. And the pronoun for that God is "he." As if to assure us that the lopsidedly masculine language is intentional, the leadership in local congregations and national church organizations is also lopsidedly male. Despite the fact that many women and men have already exited from Christianity (and Judaism) because of such gender and sexual imbalance, the exclusiveness continues.

Why?

Vernard Eller tells us why in his little book called *The Language of Canaan and The Grammar of Feminism* (Eerdmans, 1982). Because Eller uses the term *feminism* without defining what he means by it, I will try to avoid confusion by defining the word as it is used by members of the women's movement in general and Christian feminists in particular. Feminism is simply the commitment to work for the political, economic, and social equality of man and woman, boy and girl, in every area of life. To this commitment Christian feminists add the belief that mutuality— mutual submission or deference, mutual concern, mutual servanthood—is the relational order exemplified by Jesus and specified by the New Testament epistles. Therefore, if they share a commitment to human sexual equality and mutuality, men as well as women may be, and indeed are, feminists.

The trouble with the grammar of feminism, says Eller, is that it defies the language of Canaan (by which he apparently means biblical imagery and word choices). The one and only truly concrete personal word to depict the human race, Eller insists, is *man*. No other word will do because any other personal word involves specific parts of the race rather than the whole. Presenting no evidence whatsoever, Eller claims that words like *humanity* and *humankind* are impersonal, while *man* is personal and therefore absolutely irreplaceable. He thus glosses over the fact that when a word specifies a single human male (a *man*), the same word cannot truly function as generic (*man* meaning *humanity*). Even people brainwashed by eighteenth-century English grammar, people whose intellects dutifully assure them that *man* and its accompanying pronoun *he* are really generic, get a masculine picture in their imaginations when they hear and use the words.

Thus the male half of the human race comes to be understood as the norm for what humanity is all about. It should surprise nobody that women are not as good at being *man* as men are.

Nevertheless, Eller moves ahead on this basis to point out that Scripture never says that each individual human being is made in the image of God. No, only "man as a whole" is made in God's image. "God the Father" is "the ultimate paradigm of all personhood," Eller asserts, "*through* his creating of 'man' in his own image, *to* individual personhood derived from one's participation in the personhood of 'man'" (p. 14).

Furthermore, Eller tells us that the church, and "man" as the one total personal reference to the human race, is to be feminine in relationshp to "the masculinity of God (or Christ)."

Eller asserts that because the goddess-worshipping cultures surrounding Israel were more strongly male-dominated than Israel, patriarchalism posed "no bar to attributing femininity to Yahweh." He admits that "multifacetedness and variety can be attributed to God without compromising his oneness" (pp. 39–40). Thus, had the biblical authors so desired, "Israel could have come up with the concept which currently is being advanced among us [by feminists], namely, a God incorporating equally the masculine and feminine in one Person" (p. 40).

Because Eller has overlooked the biblical images of God as female, which are the subject of this book, he assumes that Israel's God is depicted as exclusively masculine, but he is without a feminine consort because the human race (*man*) is that consort. He asserts that "in Yahwism, the human race plays the role that goddesses play in the religions of dual-gendered deity." And he calls the biblical authors valiant for resisting the temptation of "moving the feminine principle into the godhead." As we shall be seeing, however, the biblical authors did indeed move the feminine principle into the godhead. For those who accept trinitarianism, it will be striking that all three persons of the divine triad are depicted in feminine as well as masculine images. So although the biblical authors are indeed valiant, it is not for the reason Eller imagines.

Although Eller admits that "whatever we say about God will *have* to be analogy," he insists that "The masculinity of God is as thoroughly rooted in the totality of scripture as any idea one could name. . . . Whatever he may be in himself, *for us* [that is, for *man*] he is Husband, Father, and King" (p. 42). By continuing to use the male pronoun, Eller, of course, implies that whatever God's ultimate self may be, that self is masculine.

Eller wrongly assumes that "feminist grammar would forbid us to think of God as masculine and thus know him as lover or father" (p. 43). Had he done his homework, he would know that the point of Christian feminists has never been that we may not know God as father or male lover, but only that we may not *stop* there. We think it short-circuits our full humanity to ignore the pluriform images of God that the Bible offers us, and therefore the multiple aspects of relating to that God.

Because of his failure to notice the biblical images of God as a natural phenomenon (*it*) or God as a female animal or as a woman (*she*), Eller claims that God "has addressed us only as his beloved, only as feminine corespondent to his own masculinity... (p. 46). He thinks that the real reason anybody would be interested in "the God beyond gender" is in order to evade "the subordination attendant upon confessing him as husband or father or lord" (p. 47). Eller's wording here flips aside the curtain to give us a quick peek at the political effects of naming God as exclusively masculine: because God is husbandlike, husbands are godlike. Because God is fatherlike, fathers are godlike. The stage is set for exploitation of girls and women.

But the chances for exploitation are severely curtailed if we go further and recognize the biblical images that say God is womanlike and motherlike, so that women and mothers are in turn godlike. The type of relationship that suggests itself when only one partner is godlike is a dominance-submission relationship. The type of relationship that suggests itself when both partners are godlike is mutuality.

Ignoring the pain of Jewish and Christian women who call for inclusive language because they no longer want to be excluded, Eller says that the call for inclusive language is simply the result of a "subjective, liberationist, human-centered" theology. Eller prefers an "objective, Barthian-type, God-centered" theology. He claims to have exposed the "smallness," the "triviality" of the "human-locked world of and for which it [the feminist grammar] would speak" (p. 56).

Remembering the Holocaust, where millions of human beings were sacrificed to Hitler's "higher truth" of "racial purity," I shudder at the concept that the human race is in any way small and trivial. The God I worship is the one described by Isaiah (57:15, RSV) who dwells "in the high and holy place, and also with [that one] who is of a humble and contrite spirit, to revive the spirit of the humble, and to revive the heart of the contrite." It is a lie to say that we love God, whom we have never seen, if we withhold help from our brothers and sisters whom we have seen (I John 4:20). While Eller no doubt means to disparage only "the human-*locked* world" that recognizes no transcendent God, surely he should be more careful of his language. The twentieth century is the great age of the martyrs. For centuries and still more in this century, people have done hideous things to each other in the name of God or some "higher truth." We need to beware of saying that anything is more important than the way we human beings treat each other.

When the National Council of Churches announced that it was recommending an inclusive language lectionary, its Commission on Faith and Order received over two thousand angry letters in a period of several months. Typical of their thrust is this letter from a male medical doctor: "God is not a feminist. God is sexist. He assigned roles to the sexes and made woman subservient to man—like it or not. Jesus picked no females for disciples. Jesus deliberately discriminated against females in accordance with the social order established by God. Thus man and woman, in the flesh, do not have equal standing before God. It is a sin to teach or program people to develop a self-image contrary to that prescribed by the Word of God."[1] Lacking Vernard Eller's sophistication and wit, this physician sets forth in crude, raw outline the disastrous results of an exclusive focus on imagery of God as male.

Accordingly, many have implicated the Bible for human cruelty. (Wordsworth, using language Eller would approve of, calls cruelty "man's inhumanity to man"). Most feminists, accustomed to hearing the Bible interpreted as Eller and the medical doctor interpret it, understandably view the Bible as the natural enemy of womankind. In *Women*,

Men, and the Bible (Abingdon, 1977), I have argued that when interpreted contextually, a theme of male-female equality and mutuality informs the book from beginning to end. Here I want to delve deeper into just one way in which the Bible supports human sexual equality and mutuality: the images of God as female that sprinkle the sacred writings of Judaism and Christianity.

NOTES

1. Quoted by Jeanne Audrey Powers (Chair, N.C.C.C. Commission on Faith and Order) in "The Image and the Images," a sermon preached at the dedication of the U.S. delegates to the World Consultation on the Community of Women and Men in the Church, March 1981. Reprint available for 70¢ from the Evangelical Women's Caucus, Box 3192, San Francisco, California 94119.

·2·

Some Lessons from History

If, indeed, images of God as female are present in the text of the Bible, it would be logical to assume that people would have noticed them long before the 1980s. And that is indeed true. I want to explore now one period of Christian history in which God was frequently spoken of in female as well as male terms, and also to mention several representatives of the many individual Christians through the ages who have read the Bible with such alertness that they have noticed and utilized the female imagery included there.

It seems most logical to me to utilize quotations from various orthodox Christian writers during discussion of the specific female God-images that are the focus of those quotations. At this point, therefore, I will simply sketch in the facts, using only a few quotations of a general nature.

After the Bible itself, some of the earliest orthodox references to a Christian mother-God occur in the second century, in the writings of Clement of Alexandria. Clement's *Paidagogos* focuses nearly a whole chapter on a maternal, suckling God. To Clement, the aspect of God's nature that has sympathy with humankind is Mother: "By his loving," Clement says, "The Father became of woman's nature." Clement also specifies that "The Word [Christ] is everything to His little ones, both father and mother. . . ."[1]

The apocryphal *Acts of Peter,* an early third-century composition, alludes to biblical images of God as female and strongly implies mutuality between God and human-kind. The following beautiful passage is addressed to Jesus Christ:

> Thou art unto me father, thou my mother, thou my brother, thou my friend, thou my bondsman, thou my steward; thou art the All and the All is in thee; and thou art, and there is naught else that is, save thee only.[2]

Like Clement, St. John Chrysostom (347–407 A.D.) uses allusions to God's motherhood in his *Homilies on the Gospel of Saint Matthew*. In his *Baptismal Instructions* Chrysostom says that "Just as a woman nurtures her offspring with her own blood and milk, so also Christ continuously nurtures with His own blood those whom He has begotten." At about the same time in the West, Saint Ambrose of Milan speaks of "the Father's womb" and even of the nourishing breasts of Christ. And in the early fifth century, the Bishop of Ptolemais in Lybya, Synesius, said of the Christian divinity, "You are Father, You are Mother, You are male, and You are female."[3]

Others in the orthodox Christian tradition who utilize one or several of the biblical images of God as female include Valentius (2nd century), Saint Gregory of Nyssa (d. about 395), Saint Augustine of Hippo (d. 430), the Venerable Bede (c. 673–735), Peter Lombard (1110–1164), Thomas Aquinas (1225–1274), St. Bonaventure (1221–1274), and St. Gregory Palamas (d. 1359). The mystical writer Mechtild von Hackeborn (d. 1298) makes reference to all three divine persons as mothers, stating that Christ in a conversation told her directly that God's love is her mother. Other Christian women sharing in the tradition of a female, maternal God include the Blessed Angela of Foligno (1248–1309), Saint Catherine of Siena

(1347–1380), Saint Bridget of Sweden (c. 1302–1373), Margery Kempe (d. after 1415), Dame Julian of Norwich (d. after 1415), and St. Theresa of Avila (d. 1582). In her *Revelations of Divine Love,* Dame Julian developed the image of a Christian feminine divinity more fully, more centrally, and more creatively than any other medieval author.[4]

It should be obvious from this list that on the whole, more men than women have explicitly recognized the feminine principle in the godhead. None of these people had been influenced by "subjective, liberationist, human-centered theology." None of them could possibly be accused of trying to evade "the subordination attendant upon confessing [God] as husband or father or lord." By utilizing imagery of God as female, they were very simply following the usage of Scripture and the guidance of their own inner experience.

Caroline Walker Bynum has pointed out that in the twelfth century, many Cistercian monks tended to use "explicit and elaborate maternal imagery to describe God and Christ." Among them were Bernard of Clairvaux (d. 1153), Aelred of Rievaulx (d. 1167), Guerric of Igny (d. about 1157), Isaac of Stella (d. about 1169), Adam of Perseigne (d. 1221), Helinand of Froidmont (d. about 1235), and William of St. Thierry (d. about 1148), all of whom were perhaps influenced by the Benedictine Anselm of Canterbury (d. 1109), who enjoyed speaking of "mother Jesus." (Long before Anselm, however, Origen, Irenaeus and others had spoken of Christ as mother.) Comments Bynum, "Descriptions of God as a woman nursing the soul at her breasts, drying its tears, punishing its petty mischief-making, giving birth to it in agony and travail, are part of a growing tendency in twelfth-century monastic writing to speak of the divine in homey images and to emphasize its approachability."[5]

Because medieval Christian theology affirmed the goodness of creation in its physicality, the Cistercians apparently felt that "a God who is mother and womb as well as father and animator could be a more sweeping and convincing image of creation than a father God alone."[6] At the same time, their usage had the advantage of being more biblical than the exclusively masculine God-image could ever be.

Professor Bynum points out that "it is not at all clear, although many scholars assume it, that women are particularly drawn to feminine imagery." Bridal imagery is more common in writing by female mystics, while men seem more attracted to married women saints, devotion to the Virgin, and the idea of a maternal God. "Thus, to some extent, males seem to have been attracted to female images and women to male images."[7]

If the God with whom male mystics wanted to unite was described in male language, it became difficult for them to utilize metaphors of sexual union. Some monks solved that problem by depicting themselves or their souls as the brides of Christ, but others did so by making God the female parent with whom they could achieve physical union in the womb or at the breast.[8]

All of this would seem to suggest that the widespread use of inclusive God-language in Christian worship might well benefit contemporary men even more than women. It is quite possible that one reason so few men attend church regularly is that they are unconsciously repelled by being called toward intimacy with an exclusively masculine God. Although Christian women are denied the psychic power of identifying with that God (unless they are willing to deny their own womanliness), at least most women are able to aspire toward intimacy with God as husband or lover without experiencing an internal shudder based on societal taboos.

Bynum's historical evidence provides us with an important warning about contemporary social changes: the use of inclusive God-language will not necessarily bring about justice for women in society or even in the church. The *female* (or woman) and the *feminine* are two different things. The female is a person of a specific gender, whereas the feminine is an aspect of a person of either gender. Therefore the attitudes of a man toward the feminine may have very little carry-over into his actions toward specific women. By exploring the feminine he may in fact be focused on his own attitudes toward himself and the need and obligation to be nurturant toward other males. Thus, the widespread twelfth-century Cistercian use of feminine references to God exists side by side with reluctance to support and assist Cistercian nuns. And Bernard of Clairvaux links receptivity to the mothering of Jesus with absolute, total repudiation of one's biological mother, citing Jerome's idea that to follow the cross a monk should be ready to tread over his prostrate mother and father.[9]

A seventeenth-century Anglican preacher and poet provides an even more dramatic example of the conjoining of Bible-based references to God as feminine, and unjust attitudes toward actual women. Because John Donne read the Bible with the precision of an artist's eye, he sometimes utilized images of God as female in his sermons. But his own attitudes remain sexist; he does not value God's "feminine" attributes as highly as the "masculine" ones. For instance, while discussing God's relationship with Israel, Donne says, "God was their father; and ... *Their Mother* too. For ... it was a Mother's part to give them *suck*, and to feed them with *temporall blessings;* It was a Father's part to *instruct* them, and to feed them with *spirituall* things; and God did both abundantly. Therefore doth God submit himself to the comparison to a *Mother* in the Prophet *Esay* [Isaiah 49:15], *Can a woman forget her sucking child?* But then he stays not in that inferiour, in that infirmer sex, but returns to a stronger love, then that of a Mother, (yes, [says he] *she may forget, yet will not I forget thee*)."[10] Plainly Donne recognizes a feminine component in the godhead but assumes that God-as-Mother is utterly inferior to God-as-Father. Hence, although he occasionally praises individual women, Donne has no qualms about teaching the inferiority of women in general to men in general.

What are the implications for twentieth-century society? One is, surely, that learning to speak of God as inclusive of both the masculine and feminine is simply not sufficient to bring about human sexual justice. Donne could preach about a "feminine," nurturant aspect of the godhead; but as long as providing physical care is judged to be inferior to providing spiritual care, many men will continue to resist household and parenting tasks and will continue to block women from positions of spiritual leadership. Jungian psychologists, who emphasize perpetual masculine and feminine principles in the human psyche, will especially need to confront the problem of value judgments. We must take pains to re-educate ourselves concerning the equal value of qualities traditionally associated with male and female, such as "masculine" logic and light, and "feminine" imagination and darkness. In some cases we may have to reject traditional associations outright—such as the notion that "masculine" is warm (solar) while "feminine" is cold (lunar). But if we can teach ourselves to value roles traditionally associated with the female on a truly equal level with those associated with the male, the result will be the enrichment of all humanity.

Inclusive God-language is a step in the direction of that enrichment. It is only a beginning, but on the other hand it *is* a beginning. Whereas many religious leaders lament their inability to do more to alleviate world hunger, the nuclear threat, and other economic and racial inequities, their own language is something they could control almost immediately. By recognizing the female presence in their grammatical choices, and by utilizing biblical references to God as female, they could demonstrate the sincerity of their commitment to human justice, peace, and love, and therefore to psychological and social health.

NOTES

1. Jennifer Perone Heimmel, *"God Is Our Mother"*: *Julian of Norwich and the Medieval Image of Christian Feminine Divinity* (St. John's University Doctoral Dissertaton, 1980; published on demand by University Microfilms International), p. 15. I am heavily indebted to this excellent study.
2. Montague Rhodes James, ed., *The Apocryphal New Testament* (Oxford: Clarendon Press, 1924), p. 335.
3. Heimmel, pp. 21–22.
4. Heimmel, *passim.* Kathryn A. Piccard has also gathered a great deal of valuable information in *Bible Images of God*, worksheets informally published by the author in 1977. For copies, send $1.00 and S.A.S.E. with a request for *Bible Images of God* worksheets to the Rev. K.A. Piccard, 28 King Street, Dorchester, MA 02122. Piccard's worksheets contain a list of 63 extra-canonical anonymous writings and individual authors utilizing biblical imagery of God as female. Some references I have discussed are also drawn, of course, from my own study of primary sources.
5. *Jesus as Mother: Studies in the Spirituality of the High Middle Ages* (Berkeley: University of California Press, 1982), p. 129.
6. Bynum, p. 134.
7. Bynum, pp. 140–141 and p. 162.
8. Bynum, p. 161.
9. Bynum, p. 145 and *passim.*
10. George R. Potter and Evelyn M. Simpson, eds., *The Sermons of John Donne*, 10 vols. (Berkeley: University of California Press, 1953–62), 7:418–419. See Virginia R. Mollenkott, "John Donne and the Limitations of Androgyny," *Journal of English and Germanic Philology*, LXXX (January 1981), 22–38.

·3·

The Godhead as a Woman in the Process of Giving Birth

More pervasive than any other biblical image of God as female is the image of a maternal deity. Not only is the Creator depicted as carrying in the womb or birthing the creation, but also Christ and the Holy Spirit are depicted in similar roles.

Isaiah 42:14 uses a simile of Yahweh's experiencing labor pains. Advancing like a hero against unjust idolators, Yahweh speaks: "From the beginning I have been silent,/ I have kept quiet, held myself in check./ *I groan like a woman in labor,*/ I suffocate, I stifle" (JB, emphasis mine). Powerfully, God's anguish at the human failure to embody justice is captured in the image of a woman writhing, unable to catch her breath in the pain of her travail. This image makes God seem very much present alongside all those who are oppressed by the turmoil and suffering of our world. Out of God's travail comes a new world in which the blind are safely led, their darkness turning to light (Isaiah 42:16).

A more serene, transcendent image of God the Mother occurs in Acts 17: 26 and 28, during Paul's speech to the Athenian Council of the Areopagus. Paul declares that God is not dependent on anything, since God is the one who has given life and breath to everyone. Furthermore, this God is not far from any of us, for it is *in God* that we live, and move, and exist. Although the apostle does not specifically name the womb, at no other time in human experience do we exist *within* another person. Thus Paul pictures the entire human race—people of all colors, all religions, all political and economic systems—as living, moving, and existing within the cosmic womb of the One God.

Such an image would not have felt outlandish to Paul, for with his solid Jewish education he would have been familiar with the reproductive image of God as both male and female in Deuteronomy 32:18: "You forget the Rock who begot you, unmindful now of the God who gave you birth."[1] He would have known that Job 38:28–29 again balances parental images, speaking of God's fathering of the rain and giving birth to the ice from her womb. He would no doubt have remembered that Job 38:8 speaks of the sea as leaping "tumultuous from the womb." Out of that all-encompassing womb God has given birth not only to all human beings, but to the whole magnificent natural creation as well.

Even more relevant to Paul's implicit womb-image in Acts 17:28 would be his awareness that the Hebrew word *rachum* or *racham*, usually translated *compassion*, is closely related to the word for womb (*racham* or *rechem*). Thus, as Phyllis Trible has suggested, Hebrew references to God's compassion could meaningfully be translated "God's womb-love."[2] Acts 17:28 can therefore be understood as assurance that all human beings exist not only within the womb, but within the yearning womb-*love*, of God the Mother.

Perhaps Jesus had all this in mind when he implied that his suffering on the cross initiated the birth-pangs or travail of bringing forth the New Humanity. He did that by using a birth image in John 16:21 (KJV) to comfort the disciples concerning the difficulties they would confront in this world. A woman, he said, has sorrow when her *hour is come* and her birth contractions begin, but later her sorrow is turned to joy by the actual arrival of the baby. According to John's account it was only minutes later that Jesus began to pray with the words, "Father, the *hour is come*" (17:1). What hour? The hour of Christ-the-Mother's pain and sorrow: the hour of the birth pangs.

Paul utilized similar images in Romans 8:22: "From the beginning till now the entire creation, as we know, has been groaning in one great act of giving birth; and not only creation, but all of us who possess the first fruits of the Spirit, we too groan inwardly as we wait for our bodies to be set free" (JB). Salvation is here depicted as a birth process occurring not only within each individual (microcosm), but also within the natural creation as a whole (macrocosm). Thinking about the image in the light of actual female experience, we remember how heavy a woman feels just before she gives birth, how eager she is to be set free from her nine months' "confinement." We also realize that tension and straining only make birthing a much more painful and difficult process. The idea in natural childbirth is to learn to relax, to breathe rhythmically, to cooperate with the body. Similarly, the process of becoming more Christ-like is eased by learning to be patient with ourselves, working in harmony with our bodies rather than punishing them for the sake of what we imagine to be spiritual progress. To paraphrase William Butler Yeats, body must not be bruised to pleasure soul.

Because Paul understood that we Christians are intended to reflect God's motherhood in the nurturance of our own spirits and of each other, he did not hesitate to use female images concerning himself. He wrote to the Christians at Galatia, "I must go through the pain of giving birth to you all over again, until Christ is formed in you" (4:19)—a double birth-image, since Paul says he would have to suffer renewed birth pangs until Christ's image had been fully conceived and gestated (formed) within the Galatians. When that had happened, of course, they could then proceed to give birth on their own.

Since Paul utilized mother-imagery in imitation of God-as-Mother, it should be no surprise to us that Cistercian abbots of the twelfth century also had no qualms about depicting their work in terms of motherhood. For instance, Bernard of Clairvaux urges prelates to "Learn that you must be mothers to those in your care, not masters."[3]

Jesus spoke of the Holy Spirit as mother in John 3:6: "What is born of the flesh is flesh; what is born of the Spirit is spirit." To be born of the flesh is to emerge from a human mother; to be born of the spirit is to emerge from the divine Mother. Similarly John's Gospel asserts that those who believe on the Word "who was not born out of human stock" will themselves "become children of God," or in other words be "born of God" (1:12). And John's First Epistle asserts that everyone who loves is "born of God" (4:7). Such passages encourage us to see all "new-birth" or "born-again" images as affirmations of the female component in the divine nature. To proclaim that people "must be born again" is to urge them to experience the womb and the birth canal of God the Mother.

What this means, practically speaking, is turning away from egocentricity and becoming as perfectly attuned to God's will as a fetus is attuned to the woman whose life supports its life. Jacob Boehme (1575–1624), the great German Protestant visionary, describes the new-birth process this way: "the life and will of sin must die, and must become as a child that knows nothing and groans only for the mother who bore it. So too a Christian's will must enter completely into its mother, as into the Spirit of Christ. . . . There will and desire are only ordered to the mother. . . ."[4] That mother, Boehme indicates, is the Word of God: "This

Word is our eternal mother in whose body we are begotten and nourished."[5] And Boehme sighs, "If we did not know half as much, and were more childlike . . . and lived as children of one mother, as twigs on one tree that all take sap from one root, we would be much holier."[6]

Indeed. The pursuit of holy peace within and the pursuit of peace on earth are perhaps the best of all reasons for lifting up the biblical image of God as the One Mother of us all.

NOTES

1. Phyllis Trible, *God and the Rhetoric of Sexuality* (Philadelphia: Fortress, 1978), p. 62. Trible points out that the Jerusalem Bible translation, "The God who fathered you," is "inadmissible."

2. For brilliant, in-depth discussion of womb-imagery in the Bible, see the chapter entitled "Journey of a Metaphor" in Phyllis Trible, *God and the Rhetoric of Sexuality*, pp. 31–59.

3. Carolyn Walker Bynum, *Jesus as Mother: Studies in the Spirituality of the High Middle Ages* (Berkeley: University of California Press, 1982), p. 118.

4. *The Way to Christ*, trans. Peter C. Erb (New York: Paulist Press, 1978), p. 140.

5. *The Way to Christ*, p. 112.

6. *The Way to Christ*, p. 166.

· 4 ·

God as Nursing Mother

The Bible depicts God as a woman not only carrying us in her womb and bringing us to birth in creation and redemption, but also as suckling that aspect of ourselves that remains always in infantlike dependency. Let us consider, for instance, Isaiah 49:15: "Does a woman forget her baby at the breast,/ or fail to cherish the son [or daughter] of her womb?/ Yet even if these forget, I will never forget you." Although this passage does not use direct simile or even metaphor, an analogy is established. God's love is like a woman's love for her suckling child—but with this difference: that even though occasionally a few human mothers may fail their children, God will not *ever* forget her little ones. To say this is not to say that motherlove is an inferior kind of love. It is only to say that human love is not able to be as constant, reliable, or consistent as divine love. Clearly the comparison of God's love with the love of a nursing mother indicates that in the author's eyes, such motherlove is the *most* constant, *most* reliable, and *most* consistent of all forms of human caring.

A similar image occurs in the eleventh chapter of Numbers. Here Moses is depicted in one of those Hebraic arguments with God that demonstrate close intimacy, since they would never occur in any other context. Because Yahweh is angry at the Israelites, Moses complains, "Why do you treat your servant so badly? Why have I not found favor with you, so that you load on me the weight of all this nation? Was it I who conceived all this people, was it I who gave them birth, that you should say to me, 'Carry them in your bosom, like a nurse with a baby at the breast' ... Where am I to find meat to give to all this people...?" (12–13). Obviously, Moses is saying that since God was the mother who conceived and gave birth to the children of Israel, then God should be the one to carry and suckle them and find meat for them to eat. Moses resents being saddled with the job of wet nurse! And apparently Yahweh sees the justice of Moses' complaint, because immediately thereafter, steps are taken to give Moses assistance in governing the people (verses 16 ff.).

The apocryphal Book of II Esdras, dating from the first century, also makes use of the image of God as a mother or a wet nurse for infants: "Thus saith the Almighty Lord, have I not prayed you as a father his sons, as a mother her daughters, and a nurse her young babes, That ye would be my people, and I should be your God...?" (1:28–29, KJV). Male and female parent-images are here balanced off to intensify God's yearning for his/her recalcitrant children.

The image of God as nursing humankind at her loving breast has always been a favorite one, especially among male Christians. For instance, Clement of Alexandria writes of "the milk flowing from the Father" and "the 'care-banishing breast' of God the Father,"[1] demonstrating the uncomfortably hermaphroditic imagery that arises when people feel stuck with a masculine deity yet experience from God what feels to them like feminine ministrations. Surely we would be wiser to use the pronoun that matches the image as we are using at the moment! Alternatively, we might be wise to avoid sex-specific pronouns when speaking of a God who is simultaneously *both* male and female, and *neither* male nor female. For instance, one of the earliest recorded Greek Christian hymns, of uncertain authorship but credited to Clement, reads as follows:

> These thy little ones
> Draw for their nourishment
> With infancy's lips
> Filling their souls
> With spiritual savor
> From breasts of the Word.[2]

St. Augustine also speaks of Christ as a nursing mother, going into detail about exactly what he means by the analogy:

> He who has promised us heavenly food has nourished us on milk, having recourse to a mother's tenderness. For just as a mother, suckling her infant, transfers from her flesh the very same food which otherwise would be unsuited to a babe (the little one actually receives that he [or she] would have received at table, but the food conveyed through the flesh is adapted to the child), so our Lord, in order to convert His wisdom into milk for our benefit, came to us clothed in flesh.[3]

One female mystic who utilizes the nursing image is Teresa of Avila. In *The Interior Castle*, she comments, "For from those divine breasts where it seems God is always sustaining the soul there flow streams of milk bringing comfort to all the people. . . ."[4] This and similar quotations would indicate that many orthodox Christians interpreted New Testament references to "milk" as the breast milk of God or Christ-as-Mother. That they are correct to do so is indicated by the most explicit of these references, I Peter 2:2–3: "You are newborn, and, like babies, you should be hungry for nothing but milk—the spiritual honesty which will help you to grow up to salvation, now that you have tasted the goodness of [Christ]." Since in biblical times *all* babies were breast-fed babies, this clearly is an image of Christ as suckling newborn Christians.

According to John 7:37, Jesus cried out, "If any man [or woman] is thirsty, let him [or her] come to me!/ Let the man [or woman] come and drink who believes in me!" And John comments, "As scripture says, from his breast shall flow fountains of living water" (John 7:38). Although a masculine pronoun is utilized, clearly the breast that gives living water is the breast of God, with which Jesus identifies himself by inviting believers to come and drink *from his very body*. The word used here in John 7:38 is *Koilia*, which means "a hollow place" and is used to refer to the upper part of the body cavity; so the word can properly be translated as "breast," as the Jerusalem Bible does. Many other translators have hesitated to project upon Jesus a maternal image, but apparently John himself did not share their fear.[5]

Frequently Christian authors have conflated breast milk and the blood of Christ, on the basis of such passages as John 6:57–58: ". . . Anyone who does eat my flesh and drink my blood/ has eternal life. . . . For my flesh is real food/ and my blood is real drink. . . ." That such passages were understood to be maternal images is illustrated by this wholly typical passage from St. John Chrysostom's *Baptismal Instructions:* "Have you seen with what food he nurtures us all? . . . Just as a woman nurtures her offspring with her own blood and milk, so also Christ continuously nurtures with His own blood those whom He has begotten."[6] Thus the Eucharist or Holy Communion becomes a drinking at the breast of God the Mother.

Guerric of Igny spoke of the Holy Spirit as the milk pouring out from the breasts of Christ, as a result of which Saul the torturer became Paul the mother: "the executioner became the nurse . . . the whole of his blood was changed into the sweetness of milk. . . ."[7] This reference to Paul as mother and wet nurse is not at all fanciful, since as we saw earlier, Paul used birthing imagery concerning himself. And in I Thessalonians 2:7-8 Paul made the comparison even more explicit: "Like a mother feeding and looking after her own children, we felt so devoted and protective toward you, and had come to love you so much, that we were eager to hand over to you not only the Good News but our whole lives as well." That Paul had observed the average mother closely is evident from his description of his own mothering activities as "slaving night and day" (verse 9).

Other biblical passages that have been understood as nursing images include Psalm 34:9 ("O taste and see that the Lord is good," KJV); and Hosea 11:4, where God is depicted as saying, "I was like someone who lifts an infant close against her cheek; stooping down to [Ephraim] I gave him his food." The interested reader may want to track down the many other places where the Bible and orthodox Christian authors touch upon God as a suckling mother; to list all of them here would be tedious. The sheer *plenty* of these references serves as a shock to a person like me, brought up in a Protestant evangelical tradition where maternal images for God were totally repressed. Although we proclaimed our absolute devotion to the Bible (the *sola Scriptura* of the Reformers), obviously there was a great deal of imagery that we missed. Much of it was the warm, intimate, affective imagery of an immanent, maternal God. No wonder we were doctrine oriented—as one wag put it, "Clear as ice and just as cold!"

The mother who suckles her infant is also responsible to wean that infant, to help her child become more independent in the world, and (as implied in Numbers 11) to help it make progress from milk to meat. The weaning image is made explicit in Psalm 131:1-2, where the Psalmist sings, "I am not concerned with great affairs/ or marvels beyond my scope./ Enough for me to keep my soul tranquil and quiet/ like a child in its mother's arms,/ as content as a child that has been weaned."

Psalm 131 seems to me a vitally important passage for activists in the Judeo-Christian tradition. If we are to avoid burnout, we must not try to do *everything* ("great affairs/ or marvels beyond our scope"). We must limit ourselves only to that for which our specific gifts have prepared us and our energy has equipped us. And we must give ourselves the leisure necessary to "keep our soul[s] tranquil and quiet." Although by taking responsibility for the world around us we have demonstrated that we have completed the weaning process in at least one part of our natures, we must allow ourselves the time to lie in the lap of God our Mother. If we are to continue to be energized and effective, we must preserve contact with that place in the center of us that despite the world's turmoil remains "tranquil and quiet ... as content as a child that has been weaned."

NOTES

1. Jennifer Perone Heimmel, *"God Is Our Mother,"* p. 18.
2. Heimmel, p. 19.
3. St. Augustine, *On The Psalms*, cited by Heimmel, p. 25.
4. Transl. Kieran Kavanaugh, O.C.D. and Otilio Rodriguez, O.C.D. (New York: Paulist Press, 1979), pp. 179–180.
5. Leonard Swidler, *Biblical Affirmations of Woman* (Philadelphia: The Westminster Press, 1979), p. 173.
6. Heimmel, p. 21.
7. Caroline Walker Bynum, *Jesus as Mother*, p. 122.

·5·

God's Other Maternal Activities

The imagery of God as giving birth to or suckling humankind, being based on biology, is unmistakably female. Other biblical images concerning God's care for dependent humanity are based on sex role stereotypes. That is, these things *could* be done by fathers or other males, and sometimes *are* done by men in our culture. But sex roles in biblical times and places assigned these jobs as exclusively "women's work," so their proper effect is to picture God as female.

My intention in pointing out the images of God's eternal childcare is certainly not to discourage fathers from assuming greatly increased responsibilities in parenting. Actually, the effect ought to work the other way around. If God can be depicted as doing lowly "female parenting" tasks, then surely no person alive is too good to "stoop" to them. Perhaps, if these images were utilized often enough, childcare tasks might even come to seem what they truly are—often difficult, but always dignified and important privileges and responsibilities.

Hosea 11:3–4 unmistakably depicts God as caring for a very difficult and disobedient child: "When Israel was a child I loved him,/ and I called my son out of Egypt./ But the more I called to them, the further they went from me. . . . I myself taught Ephraim to walk,/ I took them in my arms;/ yet have they not understood that I was the one looking after them./ I led them with reins of kindness,/ with leading strings of love." It is only fair to women to recognize in this passage the work women have done for centuries—and the patient, yearning tenderness of maternal love.

A fascinating passage in the Book of Job utilizes homey images to capture God's relationship to the ocean. Yahweh speaks to Job from the heart of the whirlwind:

> Who pent up the sea behind closed doors
>   when it leaped tumultuous out of the womb,
> When I wrapped it in a robe of mist
>   and made black clouds its swaddling bands;
> When I marked the bounds it was not to cross
>   and made it fast with a bolted gate?
> Come thus far, I said, and no farther....

Anybody who has ever dressed an energetic youngster, put diapers on a kicking, squirming child, erected barriers to keep an inquisitive toddler out of harm's way, or struggled with a playpen, should understand this amazing image. God the Mother not only gives birth to the sea, but also dresses it in mist, diapers it in black clouds, erects barriers it cannot cross, and puts it into an enormous playpen with a bolted gate!

Many biblical images picture God as the one who carries, feeds, protects, heals, guides, disciplines, comforts, washes, and clothes her human children. A few examples must suffice:

In Isaiah 46:3-4, Yahweh speaks: "Listen to me, House of Jacob ... you who have been carried since birth,/ whom I have carried since the time you were born./ In your old age I shall be still the same...." Elsewhere, Yahweh says, "I shall pour clean water over you and you will be cleansed; I shall cleanse you of all your defilement" (Ezekiel 36:25). Since women were required to do most of the cleaning up then as now, statements throughout the Bible about cleansing us from sin carry overtones of God's motherhood.

Because women were also responsible for making clothing for their families, we can recognize female connotations in Genesis 3:21: "Yahweh God made clothes out of skins for the man and his wife, and they put them on." Job 10:10–12 also refers to weaving clothes, depicting God's creation of a human being by comparison to distinctly female activities: "Did you not pour me out like milk,/ and curdle me then like cheese;/ clothe me with skin and flesh,/ and weave me of bone and sinew?/ And then you endowed me with life,/ watched each breath with tender care." The familiar statement in Luke 18 that God, who clothes the grass in the field, will also clothe us is a maternal reference, as is the statement that Christ's own personality becomes our garment when we are baptized (Galatians 3:27). The latter passage indicates one of most desirable results of the inclusive naming of God: the increased solidarity of the global human family as children of the One Father-Mother who is in Heaven. For we are told that once clothed in the garment of the Christ, the New Humanity will recognize "no more distinctions between Jew and Greek, slave and free, male and female" (verse 28).

The act of wiping away tears from the eyes (Revelation 21:4) is traditionally feminine. Isaiah 66:13–14 makes explicit the fact that such comforting often indicates the presence of God's maternal aspect, for Yahweh promises, "Like a son comforted by his mother/ will I comfort you." Again I would like to emphasize that reclaiming the femininity of these images is not intended to reinforce stereotypes of women as gentle and men as stern or unresponsive. The point of reclaiming the female component in the supposedly masculine God of the Bible is rather to affirm both the masculine and feminine components in every human being, and to honor the work which women have done through the centuries alongside the achievements of men.

In the Wisdom of Solomon, a beautiful book from the first century B.C.E. that influenced several New Testament passages, God's feeding of Israel in the wilderness is depicted as the activity of an indulgent—almost doting—mother:

> You gave them the food of angels [i.e., manna],
> from heaven untiringly sending them bread already prepared,
> containing every delight, satisfying every taste.
> And the substance you gave demonstrated your
>   sweetness toward your children,
> for, conforming to the taste of whoever ate it,
> it transformed itself into whatever the eater wished.
>
> (*The Wisdom of Solomon 16:20–21*)

Hadewijch, a mystical poet and member of the Beguines, the thirteenth-century women's movement, uses a similar image of bread from heaven as she describes God in terms of Love. Love is a courtly lady whom a masculine humanity must obey as the courtly lover obeys his mistress:

> Her name is *a-mor*, "delivered from death"—
> He whom Love touches cannot die—
> Her name is *a-mor*, "delivered from death"—
>   If he has done what Love commanded
>   And in this has failed in nothing.
>   She is the wealth of all things;
>   Love is that *living bread*
>   And above all sweet in taste.[1]

In the long text of Julian of Norwich's *Showings* (often called the *Revelations of Divine Love*), Chapters 58 through 61 are devoted almost exclusively to developing the concept that "God almighty is our loving Father, and God all wisdom is our loving Mother, with the love and goodness of the Holy Spirit, which is all one God, one Lord."[2] She specifies that the second person of the Trinity is "our Mother in nature in our substantial creation, in whom we are founded and rooted, and [Christ] is our Mother of mercy in taking our sensuality" (p. 294). By insisting that "our sensuality is only in the second person, Christ Jesus," Dame Julian highlights an important advantage in recognizing biblical images of God as female. To overemphasize God's "masculinity" is traditionally to overemphasize the abstract and the transcendent; to affirm God's "femininity" is to affirm our own humanity, our physicality, what Julian terms our "sensuality." By becoming flesh, "Mother Jesus" carried our humanity into the godhead.

Dame Julian depicts Christ as our birth-mother in creation, incarnation, and redemption. Jesus also feeds us with his own body, and continually does "the service and the office of motherhood in everything" (p. 297). Julian is very specific:

> To the property of motherhood belong nature, love,
> wisdom and knowledge, and this is God. . . .
> The kind, loving mother who knows and sees
> the need of her child guards it very tenderly, as
> the nature and condition of motherhood will have.
> And always as the child grows in age and in
> stature, she acts differently, but she does not
> change her love. And when it is even older, she
> allows it to be chastized to destroy its faults,
> so to make the child receive virtues and grace.
> This work, with everything which is lovely and
> good, our Lord performs. . . . So he is our Mother. . . .
> [When we are afraid, Christ] wants us to act as a
> meek child, saying:
> My kind Mother, my gracious Mother, my
> beloved Mother, have mercy on me. . . . The sweet
> and gracious hands of our Mother are ready and
> diligent about us; for [Christ] in all this work

exercises the true office of a kind nurse, who has
nothing else to do but attend to the safety of her
child (pp. 299, 301, and 302).

On the basis of her visions and revelations, Dame Julian
asserts that Christ wants us to know about God's motherhood (p. 299) so that our love will be fully attached to
God. That alone provides reason enough to lift up and proclaim the biblical images of God as Mother!

NOTES

1. *Hadewijch: The Complete Works*, trans. Mother Columba Hart,
O.S.B. (New York: Paulist Press, 1980), p. 132.
2. *Julian of Norwich: Showings*, trans. Edmund Colledge, O.S.A.
and James Walsh, S.J. (New York: Paulist Press, 1978), p. 293.

·6·

God as Midwife

In biblical times and places, the nearest any woman could come to respected professional status was to serve as a midwife. The first chapter of Exodus gives us a glimpse of what this work was like: two Hebrew midwives, Shiprah and Puah, regularly assisted at the deliveries of Hebrew and Egyptian women. Few of us have ever heard of Shiprah and Puah; like many other heroic women, they have not been granted sufficient credit for their courageous acts. They risked their lives by defying the orders of the king of Egypt to destroy every Hebrew boy-baby they delivered. Without their sheer nerve, Moses would have been killed at birth; and without Moses, there would have been no liberation of Israel from the slavery of Egypt. Furthermore, these women manifested shrewd wisdom in their dealings with the king. When Pharoah asked them why in fact they were not killing the Hebrew males as he had ordered, they did not confront him with their deliberate disobedience. Such confrontation would almost certainly have led to their death and the end of their usefulness. Instead, they merely commented that "The Hebrew women are not like Egyptian women; they are hardy, and they give birth before the midwife reaches them." For this strategic sidestep and for their reverence for God and human life, the midwives were rewarded with children of their own.

Several times the Hebrew scriptures compare God to a

midwife. Isaiah 66 depicts Zion as a woman giving birth to the sons who will defeat her enemies. God is the midwife at this rapid, easy birth process: "Am I to open the womb and not bring to birth?/ says Yahweh/ or I, who bring to birth, am I to close it?/ says your God" (Isaiah 66:9). God then proceeds to send "flowing peace, like a river" toward the woman called Zion, so that her babies may be "suckled, filled,/ from her consoling breast,/ that you may savor with delight/ her glorious breasts." God's ministrations toward Zion are like the acts of the midwife immediately after birth. She cleans up the infant and the mother, and then lays the newborn baby upon its mother's consoling breast to be suckled and filled.

A similar image occurs in Psalm 22:9–10. There the Psalmist addresses Yahweh in the context of feeling deserted by God and mocked by human beings. The speaker muses that despite all this, "Yet you drew me out of the womb, you entrusted me to my mother's breasts; placed me on your lap from my birth, from my mother's womb you have been my God" (JB). Since this Psalm begins with words Jesus quoted on the cross ("My God, my God, why have you deserted me?") and contains many harrowing details that well describe crucifixion, the midwife image takes on added poignancy here. We may imagine that in the hour of his own anguished "birth contractions" on the cross, Jesus tried to comfort himself by remembering that God had been the midwife drawing him out of the womb of his own mother. Since God had been with him "from my mother's womb," Jesus, like the Psalmist, may have felt justified in hoping that God would not "stand aside" now, when "I have no one to help me." Remembering that in John 16:21 and 17:1 Jesus had set up an analogy between his agony and the sufferings of a woman having birth pangs, we may be encouraged to speculate that the desertion Jesus cried out against was the desertion of the very midwife who had brought him to birth. God as midwife had seemed to absent herself from Jesus, who was enduring the torment of trying to bring forth the New Humanity.

Although it is implicit rather than explicit, there probably is a midwife image in Romans 8:26–29. The context is that the whole creation is "groaning in one great act of giving birth," and that individual Christians are also groaning inwardly, waiting for our bodies to be "set free" from their burden.

In this context we are told that "The Spirit too comes to help us in our weakness. For when we cannot choose words in order to pray properly, the Spirit . . . expresses our plea in a way that could never be put into words, and God who knows everything in our hearts knows perfectly well what [the Spirit] means, and that the pleas of the saints expressed by the Spirit are according to the mind of God."[1] The birth imagery in the context helps us get a concrete picture of what goes on when we pray. If, like a birthing mother, we get stuck and are too weak to be able to deliver in proper words the infant prayer we want to address to God, the Holy Spirit as midwife takes over and helps us to a satisfactory delivery.

The midwife image also adds great enrichment to the passage that immediately follows. "We know that by turning everything to their good God cooperates with all those who love [God], with all those that [God] has called according to [the divine] purpose. They are the ones [God] chose specially long ago and intended to become true images of [God's] Son, so that [God's] Son might be the eldest of many brothers [and sisters]" (JB, rendered inclusive by bracketed words). The masculine pronouns in English translations have perhaps blocked us from seeing that this great passage carries forward the explicit birth and implicit midwife imagery of the preceding passage. Nothing could more perfectly picture *cooperation*, indeed *co-creation*, than the human mother struggling to give birth to her new nature and the divine midwife helping her in every possible fashion. Paul returns to a family image in verse 29, saying that Jesus was the firstborn or eldest among the twice-born members of the New Humanity.

We Christians are urged, in Galatians 5:22, to give birth to the fruit or offspring of the Holy Spirit: love, joy, peace, patience, kindness, goodness, trustfulness, gentleness, and self-control. This birth process is beyond the strength and effort of the human ego when it is separated from the strength of its eternal Source. But we can always rely upon the assistance of the divine midwife. We can rest assured that she will turn everything to our good.

NOTES

1. Since the Hebrew word for Spirit is feminine, and the Greek word for Spirit is neuter, there is no earthly reason for referring to the Spirit as masculine—except for the assumption that God is masculine! I have therefore left out the Jerusalem Bible's masculine pronouns for Spirit.

·7·

The Shekinah

The word *Shekinah* derives from the Hebrew root *shkn*, meaning "to dwell." The term *Shekinah* was used by Jewish rabbis in the first or second century B.C.E. to indicate God's presence among the children of Israel—and the term was feminine in gender. Like the feminine gender terms for Holy Spirit (*Ruach Hakodesh*), voice (*Bath-Kol*), teaching (*Torah*), compassion or womb-love (*racham*), Wisdom (*Hokhma*), and Community of Israel (*Knesseth Yisrael*), *Shekinah* depicts the visible expression or residence of God's glory within the creation.

Raphael Patai explains that in both the Hebrew and Aramaic languages, the gender of a subject plays a much greater role than it does in Indo-European languages like our own. Whereas in English we could hear "The Shekinah stood up and spoke" without in any way detecting gender, in Semitic languages, because nouns, verbs, and adjectives all have separate male and female forms, both of the verbs (*stood* and *spoke*) would have been reinforcing the femininity of the feminine noun *Shekinah*. Thus, although Judaism's major names for God were masculine, and every statement about God or adjective qualifying God reinforced that masculinity by masculine forms, nevertheless the Shekinah, "with her feminine gender, comes quite close in the Talmudic sources to being regarded as a feminine manifestation of the deity."[1]

Dr. Patai wrote *The Hebrew Goddess* prior to 1967, well before the current feminist interest in reclaiming historical and biblical images of God as female, and totally unaware of the backlash that insists upon the masculinity of God in relationship to a feminine humanity. But simply as a scholarly anthropologist he asserts, "To say that God is either male or female is . . . completely impossible from the viewpoint of traditional Judaism" (p. 8). Patai knows that both Jewish and Christian theologians point out that masculine anthropomorphisms like "Lord of Hosts," "Master of the Universe," and "Our Father in Heaven" are not indicative of a literal belief in the masculinity of God. They are simply symbols that the human imagination needs to fasten upon. But at the same time Patai is sensitive to the powerful effect of imagery: "No subsequent teaching about the aphysical, incomprehensible, or transcendental nature of the deity could eradicate [the] early mental image of the masculine god [picked up from masculine expressions like Father and King]" (p. 8).

Patai admires Judaism for its creation of the world's greatest symbol and image of divine fatherhood. But as a student of comparative religions, he comments that as much as human beings need the father-image, they have "an equally great, or possibly even greater, need for yet another symbol: that of the divine woman who appears in many different forms throughout the world, yet remains basically the same everywhere" (p. 9). He treats the concept of the Shekinah, God's feminine Presence in this world, as one development arising out of Jewish craving for the divine mother.

The word *Shekinah* does not appear in the Bible, but the concept certainly does. In Exodus 24:16–18, the thick cloud enclosing the devouring flame upon Mount Sinai was understood to be the Shekinah. In Exodus 33:7–11, Yahweh descends in a cloud to talk with Moses in a tabernacle. And in Exodus 40, the cloud that rested above the tabernacle by day, and the fire that replaced the cloud during the night, were understood to be the Shekinah. When the pillar of cloud went up from over the Tabernacle, the people knew that God's Presence or Shekinah was leading them forward in their wilderness journey.

The form most closely associated with the Shekinah was "the glory of God," as in Ezekiel's statement that he "saw the appearance of the likeness of the glory of the Lord" (Ezekiel 1:28). The Targum of Onkilos, an Aramaic version of the Pentateuch prepared about C.E. 100–130, replaces "name" with "Shekinah" in Deuteronomy 12:5 so that it reads, "To the place where the Lord your God shall choose that his Shekinah may dwell there, unto the house of his Shekinah shall you seek." It also identifies the Shekinah with the angel in the story of Hagar (Genesis 16:13) and with the face of Yahweh in Numbers 6:25 and Deuteronomy 31:18. The Haggadah, the nonlegal portion of rabbinical literature, identifies the Shekinah with God's speaking to Moses in the burning bush, with the temple of Solomon, with the synagogue, and with the righteous themselves.[2]

It is significant that the Shekinah, like other feminine gender terms concerning Yahweh, focuses on Yahweh's immanence, the divine nearness to and interaction with humankind. Whereas for the Jews masculine God-language emphasized the abstract, eternal, static, transcendent nature of God, feminine terminology had to be found to express God's more everyday, humanlike, and personally affective attributes. Although the concept of the Shekinah was originally developed as a circumlocution to protect Yahweh's transcendent holiness, today many of us feel so much yearning for God's presence within human experience that we have other reasons to be grateful for the development. Rabbi Eliezer (third century) reflects both protectiveness for God's transcendence and pride in God's immanence when he says, "What 'And they saw the God of Israel' means is that they feasted their eyes on the splendor of the Shekinah."[3]

In case anyone should argue that it is only linguistic accident that Hebrew terms for God's immanent Presence within human experiences are *feminine*, it is pertinent that Luke's story of Christ's birth uses language associated with the Shekinah. Gabriel announces to Mary, "The Holy Spirit will come upon you . . . and the power of the Most High will cover you with its shadow" (Luke 1:35). The word for *overshadow* or *cover with shadow* is the same word used in the Septuagint to designate Yahweh's Shekinah glory in the tabernacle (Exodus 40:35). Its usage only helps to spotlight the central importance of the *female* in the coming of God into human flesh—that "seed of the *woman*" prophesied in Genesis 3:15 and applied to Christ in Galatians 4:4.

The Shekinah concept is also reflected many other times in the Christian Scriptures. Madeleine and J. Lane Miller see the Shekinah glory in Romans 6:4 ("raised from the dead by the Father's glory"), Hebrews 1:3 (Christ is "the radiant light of God's glory"), I Peter 4:14 (sufferers will enjoy gladness when Christ's glory is revealed), and especially in II Corinthians 4:6, which speaks of "the light of the knowledge of the glory of God in the face of Jesus Christ."[4]

It is not surprising that Saint Paul, with his rabbinical education, should have identified Christ and Christians with the Shekinah glory. For instance, in Romans Paul writes that because of sin, human beings have fallen short of "the glory of God" (3:23), but those justified by faith are able to rejoice in the hope of "sharing the glory of God" (5:2). In fact, those who behold "the glory of the Lord" are themselves transformed "from one degree of glory to another" (II Corinthians 3:18). We are reminded of the rabbinical statement in Genesis Rabbah 86:6: "Wherever the righteous go, the Shekinah goes with them."[5]

Dale Moody points out that "The fourth Gospel has so many echoes of the Shekinah glory that it has been called the 'gospel of the glory.' "[6] For instance, John 1:14 says, "The Word became flesh and dwelt among us." The word for *dwelt* is drawn from an Aramaic paraphrase of the Old Testament; it means Shekinah. The Shekinah glory of God, that "feminine" Presence, dwelt in the temple of Jerusalem; but John 1:14 together with John 2:21 asserts that the body of Jesus is now become the temple and is the perfect dwelling place of the Shekinah glory. James 2:1 carries this understanding forward to the conclusion that as Christ is, so genuine Christians ought to be. James warns that Christians should show no partiality as they hold the faith of Jesus Christ, "the Lord of Glory." In other words the presence of Christ the Shekinah within the worshipping congregation, is expected to expose the absurdity of all classist, racist, or sexist prejudices and distinctions and to do away with them.

It seems vital for contemporary people of faith to think about the implications of the fact that the Shekinah image is a feminine one. If God's immanence, perceived glory, and approachability are so often expressed through feminine images, perhaps that helps to explain the coldness, rigidity, and alienation in many congregations where female ministry is severely limited, and where exclusively masculine God-language continues to be the order of the day.

Furthermore, an overemphasis on traditionally "masculine" values can skew our perceptions in other ways. Rachel Adler, a contemporary psychotherapist and an Orthodox Jewish feminist, ponders a radical misperception that has arisen from exclusively masculine God-imagery and a corresponding focus on things quantifiable, empirical, active, and "positive." Her poem is entitled "Second hymn to the Shekinah."[7]

> Daddy says nothing
> Comes of nothing. Daddy says
> Nothing is a scalding stinking pit
> Wet lips like rotten black peonies
> Waiting to suck you in.
> Pray to Daddygod to save you, Daddy says.
>
> Lady, by all your names,
> The lost, the forgotten, the not yet born, I swear
> I'll never again
> Pray against my own flesh.
> Teach me, answer me
> Rachel to Rachel
> You tell me/ I tell you
> Nothing is my own mama and
> I am nothing myself.
>
> Open my mouth. I'll pray you
> A litany of nothing
>> hollow in the pot   nothing
>> hole in the flute   nothing
>> rest in the music   nothing
>> shabbat in the week   nothing
>> tehorn in the universe   nothing
> Amen Imi Emet
>
> I am your daughter, Lady,
> And pregnant with you.
>
> Holy wind whistle through me
> Been a long time
> Since you had a pipe for this music.

Many women who value womanhood and men who value their feminine component stand open and ready to be the instrument of Holy Lady Shekinah.

In his great elegy *In Memoriam*, Alfred Lord Tennyson wrote of the necessity of struggling with doubt as one's faith grows mature, using the image of the Shekinah:

> And Power was with him in the night
> > which makes the darkness and the light
> And dwells not in the light alone.
>
> But in the darkness and the cloud
> > As over Sinai's peaks of old. . . .[8]

As Tennyson notices, the Shekinah is both dark and light—dark cloud during bright day, and bright fire during dark night. This image, derived from biblical narrative, suggests that God's Presence is best discerned in that which is *other* from ourselves. And that in turn suggests that having been male-dominated for centuries, the churches of Christendom and the synagogues of Judaism badly need more leadership and insight from the perspective of the majority "other" always in their midst: women. Perhaps when that happens, the Shekinah will reappear splendidly among us.

NOTES

1. *The Hebrew Goddess* (New York: KTAV Publishing House, 1967, repr. Avon Books, 1978), pp. 8 and 115. Patai also includes a fascinating discussion of the cherubim that covered the Ark in the Tabernacle's Holy of Holies. Philo (20 B.C.–50 A.D.) explained that one cherub was male, the other female, to represent the male and female aspects of God. The male cherub symbolized God (*Elohim*) as Father, Husband, Begetter, Creator, Reason, Goodness, Peaceable, Gentle, and Beneficent. The female cherub symbolized the Lord (*Yahweh*) as Mother, Wife, Bearer, Nurturer, Wisdom, Sovereignty, Legislative, Chastening, and Correcting (Patai, p. 74).

2. "Shekinah," *The Interpreter's Dictionary of the Bible* (Nashville: Abingdon, 1962), Vol. IV, p. 317.

3. Cited by Patai, p. 113.

4. *The New Harper's Bible Dictionary,* Eighth Edition (New York: Harper and Row, 1973), p. 672.

5. "Shekinah," IV, p. 318.

6. "Shekinah," IV, p. 319.

7. *Response: Contemporary Jewish Review,* XIII (Fall–Winter, 1982), p. 60. Reprinted by permission of the author.

8. *In Memoriam,* no. 96, *The Norton Anthology of English Literature,* Third Edition, Major Authors Edition (New York: Norton, 1975), p. 2037.

·8·

Christic as Female Pelican

Psalm 102 has been understood by Christian exegetes as one of the Messianic Psalms. For instance, the footnote to Psalm 102 in *The New Scofield Reference Bible* states, "The reference of vv. 25–26 to Christ . . . is assurance that, in the preceding verses of this Psalm, there is shown, prophetically, the affliction of His holy soul in the days of His humiliation and rejection."[1] Part of that prophecy of Christ's affliction is an image of Christ as a female pelican, for in verse six, the afflicted and suffering speaker moans, "I am like a pelican of the wilderness." Christian tradition has not only understood the speaker to be Christ, but has understood the pelican image to specify a *mother* pelican giving her life to revive her dead offspring. The analogy is, then, that Christ is to the church as the mother pelican is to her brood.

This is a most curious image, since the bird spoken of in Scripture may not even be the pelican. Pelicans have indeed been seen in Palestine, and they make their appearance very early in Egyptian art. But the pelicans mentioned in Psalm 102, Isaiah 34:11, and Zephaniah 2:14 are associated with the wilderness and the ruins of Edom and Ninevah, places where real pelicans would not normally be found. Since these web-footed birds with enormous bills eat mainly fish, they are naturally found near swamps, estuaries, rivers, or the ocean. The biblical reference may well be to hawks, vultures, or cormorants.[2]

Since the pelican is listed among the unclean birds in Deuteronomy 14, it is most amazing that it could have come to be an image of "Mother Christ." Based entirely on the slender biblical evidence of Psalm 102:6, the image achieved popularity in the Middle Ages when it became known that Saint Gertrude of Helfta had seen a vision of Christ as a pelican.[3] But there was also the authority of Saint Jerome, who had told the story of the pelican restoring its young to life after they had been killed by serpents.[4] Sir Thomas Browne repeats this legend in the seventeenth century, and attributes it not only to Jerome, but also to "Austine, Isidore, Albertus, and many more." He credits Eucherius with being the first to call the Mother Pelican "the Emblem of Christ."[5]

The whole image was reinforced by the popular fallacy that the pelicans feed their young with their blood. In fact, when pelicans are about to feed their brood, they do macerate small fish in the large bag attached to their under-bill, then press the bag against their breast to transfer the macerated food into the mouths of the young. Medieval piety saw the pressure against the chest as a self-sacrificial bursting of the breastbone in order to provide blood for the young to drink. The fact that medieval medical theory understood breast milk to be processed blood also undergirds the pelican image of "Mother Jesus."[6]

More relevant to our theme is the medieval legend about the dying and restoration of the youthful pelicans. A twelfth-century Latin Bestiary puts it this way:

> The Pelican is excessively devoted to its children. But when these have been born and begin to grow up, they flap their parents in the face with their wings, and the parents, striking back, kill them. Three days afterward, the mother pierces her breast, opens her side, and lays herself across her young, pouring out her blood over the dead bodies.
>
> In the same way, Our Lord Jesus Christ . . . begets

and calls us into being out of nothing. We, on the contrary, strike him in the face. As the prophet Isaiah says, "I have borne children and exalted them and they have scorned me." We have struck him in the face by devoting ourselves to the creation rather than the creator.

That was why he ascended into the height of the cross, and, his side having been pierced, there came from it blood and water for our salvation and eternal life.[7]

Since the medieval *Bestiary* was a serious work of natural history, a compilation or naturalist's scrapbook drawing together information from many sources including the church fathers, its influence was tremendous. Some scholars think that because the *Bestiary* was copied and translated from one language to another, century after century, its influence was almost as widely diffused as the Bible's.

Medieval heraldry used the pelican as one of its favorite ecclesiastical symbols. Sir Thomas Browne indicates the popularity of the image in antiquity, saying that "in every place we meet with the picture of the Pelican, opening her breast with her bill, and feeding her young ones with the blood distilling from her."[8] The bird was usually shown standing above the nest, her wings outstretched, the young eating from her breast. And the blazon accompanying the depiction was "A Pelican in its Piety."[9] Since *piety* carries the classical meaning of "filial devotion," the heraldic blazon indicates the identification of Christ with the act of the mother pelican. Christ feeding us with blood (an obviously eucharistic symbol) is simultaneously a mother toward humankind and a filial Son toward the Heavenly Parent.

The most common version of the pelican legend specifies that it is the *male* bird who kills the brood;[10] and it is unanimous that it is the *female* bird who after three days returns to the nest to revive the brood by the warmth of her body and the shedding of her blood. As T. H. Huxley once commented, "Ancient traditions, when tested by the severe processes of modern investigation, commonly enough fade away into mere dreams: but it is singular how often the dream turns out to have been a half-waking one, presaging a reality."[11] The dream that the male pelican kills its offspring, while the female pelican bestows new life upon them, turns out to presage a reality for many of us in the contemporary faith-community. Exclusively male images of God are killing our spirit by distorting our understanding of masculinity, femininity, and mutuality. The recognition of biblical images of God as female, the infusion of positive female images into the language of faith, the achievement of balance between male and female references, will do a lot to bring us renewed health.

As John Skelton wrote in his early sixteenth-century poem "Armory of Birds,"[12]

> Then said the Pelican,
> When my birds be slain
> With my blood I them revive.
> Scripture doth record,
> The same died our Lord,
> And rose from death to life.

NOTES

1. (New York: Oxford University Press, 1967), p. 648.
2. "Pelican," *The Interpreter's Dictionary of the Bible* (Nashville: Abingdon, 1962), Vol. 3, p. 710.
3. Gertrude Grace Sill, *A Handbook of Symbols in Christian Art* (New York: Collier Books, 1979), p. 25.
4. William Rose Benét, "Pelican," *The Reader's Encyclopedia* (New York: Thomas Y. Crowell, 1948), Vol. III, p. 835.
5. *The Prose of Sir Thomas Browne*, ed. Norman J. Endicott (Garden City, New York: Doubleday, 1967), p. 216.
6. Caroline Walker Bynum, *Jesus as Mother* (Berkeley: University of California Press, 1982), p. 132.

7. *The Bestiary: A Book of Beasts,* trans. by T. H. White (New York: G. P. Putnam's Sons, 1954, repr. 1960), pp. 132–3.

8. *The Prose of Sir Thomas Browne,* p. 215.

9. *The Bestiary,* p. 133.

10. Benét, p. 835; Sill, p. 24.

11. *The Bestiary,* title page.

12. As quoted by William Rose Benét, p. 835.

·9·

God as Mother Bear

To the biblical authors, one of the worst fears imaginable was to encounter a mother bear whose offspring had been killed or taken from her. II Samuel 17:8 describes David and his mighty warriors being "as angry as a wandering bear robbed of her cubs." Proverbs 17:2 opines that it is better to "come on a bear robbed of her cubs/than on a fool in his folly"—implying that the only thing more dangerous than foolishness is a bereaved mother bear.

Against this background the significance of the female God-image in Hosea 13:8 stands out more clearly. That passage portrays Yahweh's comments about the punishment of those who have no gratitude for their deliverance from slavery. Since their hearts have become proud and they have forgotten God, Yahweh says,

> Very well, I will be a lion to them,
> a leopard lurking by the way;
> *like a bear robbed of her cubs I will pounce on them,*
> *and tear the flesh around their hearts;*
> the dogs shall eat their flesh,
> the wild beasts tear them to pieces.

In this very fierce image of God the Mother, human gratitude for liberation is depicted as the cubs to which the mother bear is profoundly attached. Bereaved of human gratitude, Yahweh turns in rage upon those who have "sto-len her cubs" by withholding their thankfulness. The image of internal ripping and tearing well captures the bit-ter sensations associated with fragmentation and alienation from the Source of our being. When we allow ourselves to become ungrateful for the gift of life and the liberation of faith, we often feel torn to pieces.

II Kings 2:24 reinforces the fierceness of the female bear image. When a gang of boys was jeering at the prophet Eli-sha for being bald and yelling at him to get out of their neighborhood, Elisha cursed them in the name of Yahweh: "And two she-bears came out of the wood and savaged forty-two of the boys." While the text does not actually identify the she-bears with Yahweh as Hosea does, clearly they are the agents of Yahweh's rage. Taking this passage literally no doubt runs our blood cold, since being muti-lated by bears is hardly an appropriate punishment for childish name-calling. Nevertheless the story is deeply meaningful when viewed as a myth. It is like the Greek myth of Actaeon, who reacted to the Goddess Diana (Ar-temis) as if she were simply a beautiful woman. Because he had not recognized divinity when he saw it, Actaeon was transformed into a deer and torn to pieces by the hounds belonging to Diana. Similarly, for failing to respect the persons of God's prophets (who also symbolize faith, hope, and high aspirations), human beings are punished by inner fragmentation, being buffeted by our own illusions, desires, and sensations.

Hence, in the various holy books of world religions, bears symbolize "passions or illusions which hug the mind and stifle effort." Immanuel Swedenborg took the idea a bit further by saying that "Bears signify fallacies—the literal sense of the Word, read indeed, but not understood."[1]

In the light of such unfavorable connotations, why would Hosea depict Yahweh as an enraged, bereaved

Mother Bear? Clearly Hosea was not thinking of the negative connotations of bears, but rather of the tremendous affection of the mother bear for her cubs. The medieval scientific understanding was that the bear cubs were born as little white pieces of pulp, which are subsequently arranged by the mother's constant licking into creatures "with the proper legs and arms." Alexander Pope alluded to this process in his poem the *Dunciad:*

> So watchful Bruin forms, with plastic care,
> Each growing lump, and brings it to a bear.

And Sir Thomas Browne provided a physician's explanation for how the legend got started. When the cub is born, he explained, a thick, tough membrane obscures its formation. Because the dam bites and tears this membrane asunder, an uninformed observer might understandably think that the bearcub began as an unformed lump of flesh that was given shape only by "the mouthing of the dam."[2]

Since the bear is associated with the constellation of Ursa Major, a constellation that never sets, the bear could also be associated with the constant watchfulness of Yahweh-the-Mother. In his poem "Il Penseroso" John Milton expresses a desire often to "outwatch the *Bear*," meaning to work throughout the night. Thus Hosea's bear-image may be understood to connote God's constant alertness.

The negative and positive connotations of bears seem to converge in Hosea's image, since it is human failure to recognize our debt to God—the egocentric delusion of independence from the divine Source—that causes Yahweh-as-Mother-Bear to become enraged at us. Having carefully licked the whole creation into shape, Yahweh is not passive about being robbed of the cubs of gratitude!

Understandably, Hosea's image of an infuriated female God has never achieved the popularity of the gentler, more

sentimental imagery of God as a loving and self-sacrificial
Mother. Male writers have almost always associated female
God-images with stereotypically feminine nurturance and
supportiveness. It is in female mystics, especially Gertrude
of Helfta, that we find female God-images associated with
discipline and authority as well as with tenderness. Caroline Walker Bynum makes an interesting connection between monastic life, strong female self-image, and inclusive
God-language: "Women who grew up in [medieval] mon-
asteries were less likely to be influenced by the contemporary stereotype of women as morally and intellectually inferior. Such women were likely to see themselves as
functioning with a full range of male and female, governing
and comforting roles, paralleling the full range of the oper-
ations of God."[3] Although Gertrude herself is a tougher
disciplinarian than Mechtild of Hackeborn, "both women
see the Lord of the universe, the Virgin, the saints, *and*
themselves as characterized by a very wide range of opera-
tions. . . . Mothering is a more tender image to Mechtild
than to Gertrude, but so is paternity. Fathers feed and con-
sole, as do mothers; mothers teach, as do fathers; the full
range of such images applies both to God and to self. God is
mother, emperor, and pope; Mary is mother and queen;
Mechtild herself is a prince leading an army, a preacher, a
conduit for grace, a parent to her children."[4]

Precisely because the image of God as a savagely angry
Mother Bear breaks all our stereotypes of how a woman
(especially a mother) ought to behave, it is an important
image for our time. Many women are struggling with their
anger at a society and a religion that do not appreciate the
full range of their gifts and relegates them always to a supportive, secondary, or self-sacrificial role. Yahweh's anger
at ingratitude may be viewed as a biblical authentication of
their anger.

One-way servitude is not healthy, whether it be that of

the divine Mother or the human female. The image of God as Mother Bear may be taken, then, as a warning about the need for mutuality, for a *two-way* flow of energy. If all we can offer to each other is gratitude, then we had better offer that; but the Bible makes clear that the kind of gratitude Yahweh desires of us is the doing of justice in our personal relationships and in the structures of the society we inhabit. Although many people have imagined that the Bible always depicts humanity as feminine in relationship to a masculine God, Hosea's image depicts a Mother God turning in nonstereotypical rage at an ungrateful, unjust humanity.

A Spanish Protestant Bible published at Basle in 1569 is called the "Bear Bible" because imprinted on the title page is a woodcut depiction of a bear. Whatever the publishers may have had in mind, perhaps it would prod us all toward the doing of justice to look at the Bible and see upon it Hosea's image of the demanding Mother Bear named Yahweh.

NOTES

1. G. A. Gaskell, "Bears," in *Dictionary of All Scriptures and Myths: A Classic Reference Guide to the Sacred Language of the Religions of the World* (New York: Avenel Books, 1960; repr. 1981), p. 94.

2. *The Bestiary: A Book of Beasts,* trans. T.H. White (New York: Capricorn Books, 1954; repr. 1960), pp. 45–47.

3. *Jesus as Mother* (Berkeley: University of California Press, 1982), p. 185.

4. Bynum, pp. 225–6.

·10·

The God of Naomi

In *Image-Breaking/Image-Building*, the editors announce that this *Handbook for Creative Worship with Women of Christian Tradition* (their subtitle) seeks "the God of Sarah as well as the God of Abraham, the God of Rebekah as well as the God of Isaac—the God, too, of our mothers, sisters, grandmothers, and aunts. The search itself is a form of worship. It is a response to the awareness that God's image is both male and female."[1] In this chapter I propose to consider the God Ruth saw imaged in her mother-in-law, Naomi. This image is different from most of the figures of speech discussed elsewhere in this book. Most of them are specific comparisons—similes or metaphors or analogies that appear once or more in the Hebrew or Christian Scriptures. But God-in-Naomi is an image that arises instead out of the circumstances of an entire narrative. Nevertheless, what eventually emerges is yet another image of God as female.

One of the most beautiful instances of human bonding in all of literature occurs between Ruth, a young woman, and her much older mother-in-law, Naomi. "Do not press me to leave you or to turn back from your company," says Ruth, for

wherever you go, I will go,
wherever you live, I will live.
Your people shall be my people,

and your God, my God.
Wherever you die, I will die,
and there I will be buried.
May Yahweh do this thing [that is, something
  serious] to me
and more also,
if even death should come between us!

Phyllis Trible points out that the description of Ruth as clinging (*dbq*) to Naomi (1:14) and saying "Intreat me not to abandon (*zb*) you" echoes the narrator's words concerning the male's abandoning (*zb*) his father and mother to cleave (*dbq*) to his wife in Genesis 2:24.[2] So the church has been right all along to use Ruth's words frequently as part of marriage ceremonies. Even though the commitment is from one woman to another, it is more powerful than many wedding vows. Most vows end with death, whereas this one asserts that even death will not drive a wedge between Ruth and Naomi. As Trible comments, "Not even Abraham's leap of faith surpasses this decision of Ruth's. . . . Not only has Ruth broken with family, country, and faith, but she has also reversed sexual allegiance. A young woman has committed herself to the life of an old woman rather than to the search for a husband. . . . One female has chosen another female in a world where life depends upon men."[3]

Perhaps the most fascinating thing about Ruth's decisive statement is that Ruth unequivocally accepts Naomi's God as her own. On what basis does she take such an extraordinary step? After all, Naomi and Elimelech had come to live in Moab years before without feeling any need to abandon the God of Judah. Going to live with Naomi in Judah would not have *necessitated* a change of religion; privately Ruth could have worshipped the deities of Moab. What motivated Ruth to include allegiance to Naomi's God as part of her allegiance to Naomi?

Searching the narrative, all we learn is that Ruth had

been married for a decade or so to one of the sons of Naomi
and Elimelech. (Notice that the sons are identified as *his*
sons [Ruth 1:2] until Elimelech's death, after which they
are called *her* sons [1:3]. This may well remind us of many
women in our patriarchal society who never seem to become interesting individuals with well-defined personal
identities until after their husbands have died. Only a careful practice of mutuality, with men loving their wives as
they love their own male flesh [Ephesians 5] can provide a
hedge against such misfortune).

Ruth apparently had married one of Naomi's sons after
Elimelech's death, and lived in kindness with him until he
and his brother (Orpah's husband) both followed their father in death. Hence we can assume that Ruth had known
her mother-in-law only during Naomi's exile in Moab,
only during Naomi's widowhood, and for a period of ap-
proximately ten years.

Ruth, as a native of Moab, would have been accustomed
to the worship of the gods Chemosh and Ashtorchemosh,
and to the widespread use of fertility rites exalting a variety
of gods and goddesses. What did she really know of the one
God whom she vowed henceforth to accept as her only
God, refusing to return, as Orpah had, "unto her people,
and unto her gods" (1:15)?

The text of Ruth's commitment to Naomi indicates that
Ruth gave her heart to the God imaged for her in the flesh
of her aging, widowed mother-in-law. Ruth's vow was
nine-fold: I will (1) stay with you, (2) follow you, (3)
travel with you, (4) lodge with you, (5) relate with those
to whom you relate, (6) worship the God you worship, (7)
die with you, (8) be buried with you, (9) continue to stay
with you even after death. Right in the midst of the eight
"horizontal" items—the eight promises concerning human
relating—comes the one "vertical" item, the promise concerning relationship to the Ultimate Being. Since all the

eight "horizontal" items center upon Naomi, it makes sense that the one "vertical" item also centers upon Naomi. In other words, Ruth converts from polytheism to monotheism and gives her life-long faith to a God she has seen chiefly in the image of an older woman, because of her love for that woman and her utter dedication to that woman. We may presume that her husband had also imaged for Ruth the One God worshipped by the Judeans, but Ruth does not mention him at all during her vow of fidelity to Naomi.

It is important to notice that when Noami refers to God in 1:20–21, she names God with the Hebrew name *Shaddai*, a name which can be understood as "the God with Breasts,"[4] although it is usually translated "the Almighty" or "the LORD." This reference underscores the logic of my assumption that for Ruth, Naomi had been an embodiment or incarnation of the One God as *the God with Breasts.*

At the time Ruth commits herself to her mother-in-law, Naomi is a person of no status whatsoever. From being a wife with sons, Naomi is reduced to being a widow and finally being a woman with neither husband nor sons—a nonentity in a patriarchal society. Her "nothingness" is indicated by the way the narrator refers to her as "the woman" in 1:5. Namelessness is the most obvious of all signs of powerlessness. So the God who is imaged by Naomi is a God identified with powerlessness, emptiness, nonentity. Ruth chooses to worship the God of the oppressed, not the God of the elite and fortunate.

Naomi's birth-name, probably the feminine form of Naaman, means "pleasant one" or "sweet one." But when she returned to Bethlehem bereft of her husband and sons, she asked to be called Mara, "bitter one." Taken together, these two names suggest that the God she imaged for Ruth (and for us) is truly an all-encompassing Being. Both sweet

and bitter, Naomi and Mara, this woman incarnated the
God who not only forms light but creates darkness, not
only makes good fortune but creates calamity (Isaiah 45:7).

In line with the attitudes of a patriarchal society toward
a manless woman, attitudes she had internalized, Naomi
did not think very highly of herself. Consequently she did
not believe that Orpah and Ruth would really profit by returning to Judah with her and embracing the God she worshipped. Hence Orpah returned to seek a husband among
her own people and to worship the multitudinous deities of
Moab. As is always the case, underestimation of oneself
leads to underestimation of others. Not only did Naomi
undervalue the God of Judah by urging Ruth and Orpah's
return to Moab, but she also undervalued Ruth, even after
Ruth's amazing commitment to her. In 1:21, Naomi
claimed that she was returning to Bethlehem empty,
whereas she was actually returning with a dual blessing:
her own life and Ruth's companionship and infinite poten-
tial. Naomi had fully internalized her society's judgment
that a manless woman is an empty woman.

Nevertheless, Naomi with all her limitations remained
for Ruth the image-bearer of the undivided One God who
births and breast-feeds the universe. In cooperation, Ruth
and Noami went to work on Boaz, conniving to find ways
to get him to fulfill his responsibility toward them. As Trible comments, "In their own right the women shape their
story" (p. 180). And although Boaz begins by asking a
truly patriarchal question about Ruth ("To whom does
this young woman belong?" [2:5]), through judicious
planning Naomi and Ruth soon bring him to the point
where he recognizes Ruth as a person rather than a possession ("Who are you?" [3:9]).[5]

In return for Naomi's embodiment of the divine image,
Ruth later gave into Naomi's care a baby named Obed,
who was to Naomi "a comfort to [her] and the prop of her

old age" (4:15). And Ruth, from the perspective of Judeans the wrong race (the Moabites were outcasts), the wrong class (so poor she had to collect leftovers in the fields), and the wrong sex (a woman in a man's world), is proclaimed as "better to [Naomi] than seven sons" (4:16). Thus the Book of Ruth becomes the Galatians 3:28 of the Hebrew Scriptures, depicting a triumph over the barriers of racism, classism, and sexism. Best of all, because of her devotion to the God she had seen in Naomi, Ruth the Moabitess became the great-grandmother of King David and one of the foremothers of "Jesus, who is called Christ" (Matthew 1:5-16).

NOTES

1. Edited by Linda Clark, Marian Ronan, and Eleanor Walker (New York, The Pilgrim Press, 1981), p. 12.
2. Phyllis Trible, *God and the Rhetoric of Sexuality* (Philadelphia: Fortress Press, 1978), p. 197.
3. Trible, p. 173.
4. So claims F. Cross, in *Canaanite Myth and Hebrew Epic* (1973) pp. 54-5. See Phyllis Trible, "God, Nature of, in the Old Testament," *The Interpreter's Dictionary of the Bible*, Supplementary Volume, p. 368.
5. Trible, p. 183.

·11·

God as Female Homemaker

Psalm 123 is centered upon the human visual sense, the eyes of those who are enduring difficult times. "I will life my eyes to you,/to you who have your home in heaven," cries the Psalmist. (Perhaps Jesus had this Psalm in mind when he taught us to pray to "our Father who art in heaven." Surely the point of Jesus' teaching was that we are to petition God as a personal, parental Being rather than an impersonal Force—*not* to establish God's masculinity).

Psalm 123 has in fact been christened the *Oculus Sperans* (the Eye of Hope) because of its emphasis on *looking* to the One who is in Heaven. As if to help us identify that One more precisely so that we can relate to that One more perfectly, the Psalmist gives us two similies. We are to lift our eyes to Yahweh at home in heaven in two ways: first, like the eyes of slaves fixed on their master's hand; and second, "like the eyes of a slave girl/ fixed on the hand of her mistress." Who is this mistress of the household to whom we human beings look for guidance, assistance, and compassion? Psalm 123:2 makes the answer clear:

> like the eyes of a slave girl
>> fixed on the hand of her mistress,
> so our eyes are fixed on Yahweh our God. . . .

Yahweh is, then, not only our Father and Master who is in heaven, but also our Mother and Mistress who is in heaven. If anyone needs any scriptural authorization to address the Lord's prayer to both Father and Mother, Psalm 123:1–2, with its male-female parallelism concerning the divine, would seem to provide that sanction. The addition would not constitute a judgment on the teaching of Jesus, as if he should have said "Our Father and Mother" in the first place. Because Jesus was living in a patriarchal culture, calling for truly *stupendous* changes, he had to speak in terminology that the people could grasp. The more unfamiliar and radical the concept, the more familiar and unthreatening the language had better be! Jesus *modelled* the full equality of males and females;[1] to have introduced *directly* a female image of God would at the time have been misunderstood as a reversion to paganism's multiplicity of divinities. Jesus did utilize word-pictures of God as female, as this book is in the process of demonstrating. But one good thing about word-pictures is that their significance does not dawn upon anybody who is not ready or able to receive them. Jesus' cultural surroundings made "Our Father and Mother in heaven" an impossibility; our cultural surroundings make it not only possible but necessary. With the advantage of the whole Hebrew and Christian Scriptures to guide our thinking, we are enabled to understand that recognizing Yahweh's female component is not a reversion to paganism, but rather a deepening toward a fuller and healthier orthodoxy.

The image in Psalm 123:2 is that of God as a female homemaker—a "housewife," to utilize the faulty modern terminology that sounds as if women are married to their houses. Being a homemaker in biblical days could, however, be similar to corporate management in our time. Households were often very extended and might include a retinue of several hundred people, counting all the wives and concubines and their children and servants, and all the parents and grandparents and brothers, sisters, aunts, uncles, and their offspring and servants! The "first wife" of the major man in such a retinue would have a heavy administrative responsibility. Yahweh is being compared to such a woman—the kind of woman who "gets up while it is still dark/giving her household their food,/ giving orders to her serving girls" (Proverbs 31:15).

In fact Psalm 123:2 gives us permission to see in Proverbs 31 a full-scale description of Yahweh as the perfect female homemaker, the perfect wife to a humanity which is cast by this image into a masculine role. The perfect wife is concerned for her own extended household ("all her servants [are] warmly clothed," Prov. 31:21). But she is also concerned for those beyond her own circle: "She holds out her hand to the poor,/ she opens her arms to the needy" (31:20). She is not silently subordinate, but is known for her articulated wisdom: "When she opens her mouth, she does so wisely;/ on her tongue is kindly instruction" (31:26). And the Proverbs author says, "Give her a share in what her hands have worked for" (31:31). God as perfect homemaker wants the honor and financial rewards due to her hard work; so do human homemakers! Because Yahweh as homemaker has so ably taken care of the domestic matters, humankind (her husband) is free to work in politics and government: "Her husband is respected at the city gates [where government responsibilities were carried out],/ taking his seat among the elders of the land" (31:23). In other words, from the angle of Proverbs 31, because Yahweh our Homemaker has provided us with the world to live in and the clothing of our flesh and the instruction of her Word, we are expected to take on our responsibility to bring about justice in human society.

From the angle of Psalm 123, however, we are expected to be the slaves of Yahweh, who is both our "master" and our "mistress." Although obedience to the will of Yahweh is part of this image, the Psalmist seems to be concentrating on the divine master/mistress as role-model rather than as boss. Afraid in the midst of adversity, the male and female slaves keep their eyes fixed on the *hand* of their master or mistress in order to know what to do next. It is important for contemporary women to have a *female* role model within the godhead, and Psalm 123 provides just such a role model. Throughout the centuries of patriarchy, religious women have been told to model themselves after the exclusively masculine models of the Father, Son, and (male) Holy Spirit. The masculinizing results are evident in various historical eras. For instance, ascetic women in the late Patristic age were regularly compared to Thecla, the legendary disciple of Saint Paul, who cut her hair like a man, traveled with the apostle disguised as a man, and refused to let any threats from her family or the state stop her from pursuing her vocation.[2] While we can be thankful for the courage of Thecla, her example does nothing for contemporary women who want to serve God without denying our womanliness. The revival of the Psalmist's image of Yahweh as role-model for her female slaves will be helpful to those contemporary women who want to serve God actively, but without masculinizing themselves.

Perhaps Jesus had Psalm 123 in mind when he told a story about a female homemaker who clearly is identified with the godhead. The story is recorded in Luke 15, which depicts Jesus as telling three stories to the tax collectors, sinners, scribes, and Pharisees who were gathered around. The first story is about the lost sheep, which the shepherd searches for relentlessly, despite the fact that he already has ninety-nine sheep safe within the fold. The third story is the familiar story of the prodigal son. The story wedged between these two is the story of a woman who lost one of her valuable silver coins, which she sought for relentlessly, despite the fact that she still had nine others safe within her keeping. In all three stories the conclusion is rejoicing because of the finding of what was lost.

But in stories one and two, the lost sheep and the lost coin are identified as symbolizing sinners, and the finding of them symbolizes repentance. Therefore the rejoicing that takes place is directly compared to rejoicing in heaven, among the angels of God (Luke 15: 7 and 10). And in this way we are led to the recognition that the *finder* in each case is compared to none other than God. God is like the shepherd who finds his lost sheep; and in story three, God is like the father who welcomes home his wastrel son. Therefore, God is also like the woman who finds her lost coin. " 'Rejoice with me,' she would say, 'I have found the drachma I lost.' In the same way, I tell you [says Jesus], there is rejoicing among the angels of God over one repentant sinner."

Why have we not heard more about the fact that Jesus compared God to a woman? Perhaps the handling in a one-volume Bible commentary by Charles John Ellicott will demonstrate what has happened. Ellicott notices that the lesson in the parable of the silver coin is "identical with that of the Lost Sheep," and that the drachma (coin) is "a symbol of the human soul." He also notices that "A woman seeks, not a man." But he says not a word about the fact that Jesus is depicting God as a woman. He simply mentions that Jesus was trying to attract the interest of his female listeners who would not be able to relate to shepherding but could certainly relate to a domestic dilemma like the loss of a valuable coin.[3] That's true enough, of course—but it overlooks the fact that Jesus was also affirming and empowering human females by allowing them the same privilege accorded to males: to see their own nature represented in the godhead.

All of us approach any written text with certain expectations, and those expectations govern what we are able to see in what we are reading. Perhaps it is helpful to think in terms of an interpretative grid, a grid that gives clear focus on some things and blocks us from seeing others. A patriarchal interpretative grid has simply made it impossible for most people through the ages to be able to perceive the many images of God as female which are the subject of this study. Or, as Leonard Swider puts it, "an underlying widespread Christian deprecatory attitude toward women ... blinded most Christian theologians and commentators to the strong feminism of Jesus in the Gospels."[4]

It has been suggested that the three stories in Luke 15 should be interpreted in a Trinitarian fashion. Since Jesus identified himself as the Good Shepherd, the first story would refer to the Christ. And throughout Christian history the father in the third story has been identified with God the Father. Logic would then seem to dictate that the woman seeking her lost coin would be an image of the Holy Spirit, to complete the Trinitarian formula.[5]

However, my own sense is that it is more in accordance with biblical imagery as a whole to interpret all three stories as depicting a godhead that is properly understood as both masculine and feminine (and simultaneously as neither masculine nor feminine). To depict the godhead as containing two male persons and one female person is politically unwise, since it leaves the female forever outvoted in a two-to-one power bloc. (It may sound facetious to speak of a power struggle within the godhead, but women's experience in patriarchy has taught us to be wary about the images we use.) More importantly, from the standpoint both of good literary interpretation and good theology, it is best to follow the overall usage of Scripture, which is to attribute both male and female characteristics to the divine One. It is patriarchy that has caused the female God-imagery of the Bible to be as scarce as it is (compared to male imagery). But it is universality and inspiration that has caused female God-imagery to be included at all in the sacred texts, despite the constricting patriarchal culture from which they sprang. And it is the job of those of us who care about justice for women today to make full use of what images of God as female *are* available to us in the Bible.

It is interesting that Jesus' depiction of God as a woman has to do with money. Certainly in Western civilization, money is power. Although money is frequently denigrated in biblical terms as "filthy lucre," the fact is that every cause and organization must seek for funding before any positive effect can be achieved. Although women did in Jesus' day and do still in our time make up a majority of those living below the poverty line, Jesus associates women with the possession of money and therefore with the possession of power. To those of Jesus' listeners who had "ears to hear," it must have seemed fresh and stereotype-smashing to hear Jesus talking about God as a woman—and a woman with money of her own! And in contemporary society, where the average American woman still makes about 59 cents for every dollar earned by a man, it will still seem fresh and stereotype-smashing when this parable is proclaimed.

Although Anglican poet George Herbert does not specify a female, he is fond of imaging God as a cosmic home-maker, using imagery that was certainly female-associated in the seventeenth century. For instance, in "Providence" he addresses God with these words,

> Thy cupboard serves the world: the meat is set,
> Where all may reach: no beast but knows his feed
>   (lines 49–50).

A few stanzas later, the "housewife" image returns:

> And as thy house is full, so I adore
> Thy curious art in marshalling thy goods
>   (lines 93–94).

In "The Familie," Herbert prays that his heart may be delivered from its "loud complaints and puling fears," comparing his own inner being to a house the Lord keeps:

> But, Lord, the house and familie are thine,
>   Though some of them repine.
> Turn out these wranglers, which defile thy seat:
>   For where thou dwellest all is neat (lines 5-9).

And in "Affliction (I)" Herbert uses much imagery that seems to imply a female component in God, though he is not explicit about that; but certainly he depicts God as a homemaker. God "entices" the speaker and at first gives the speaker "milk and sweetnesses," and a "sweetened pill" to dissolve rage. Newly converted, the speaker says,

> I looked on thy furniture so fine,
>   And made it fine to me:
> Thy glorious household-stuffe did me entwine
>   And 'tice me unto thee (lines 7-10).

Finally, after Herbert describes many afflictions, the image of slave and household administrator (from Psalm 123) surfaces. Dissatisfied, feeling useless, the speaker decides to leave God's household service, only to realize that without God, life is hellish:

> Well, I will change the service, and go seek
>   Some other master out.
> Ah my deare God! though I am clean forgot
>   Let me not love thee, if I love thee not (lines 63-66).[6]

In the service of God the cosmic homemaker, poet-priest George Herbert found perfect freedom.

And so, of course, may all of us. According to Jesus, God is like a female homemaker, an aggressive seeker for whatever is lost, an active woman who possesses money and power in her own right. According to the Psalmist, God is like a woman who administrates a large household staff and provides a role-model for her servants. It's our job to see to it that the religious community knows and never again forgets all that!

NOTES

1. For specifics see Leonard Swidler, *Biblical Affirmations of Woman* (Philadelphia: Westminster Press, 1979), and *Women in Judaism* (Metuchen, New Jersey: Scarecrow Press, 1976); Letha Scanzoni and Nancy Hardesty, *All We're Meant to Be* (Waco, Texas: Word Books, 1974); Virginia R. Mollenkott, *Women, Men, and the Bible* (Nashville: Abingdon Press, 1977); and other works listed in these volumes.

2. Thecla's story is recorded in the apocryphal *Acts of the Apostles*. See Rosemary Ruether, "Mothers of the Church," in *Women of Spirit: Female Leadership in the Jewish and Christian Traditions*, ed. Rosemary Ruether and Eleanor McLaughlin (New York: Simon and Schuster, 1979), p. 74.

3. *Ellicott's Bible Commentary in One Volume*, condensed by Donald N. Bowdle (Grand Rapids, Michigan: Zondervan Publishing House, 1971), p. 788.

4. *Biblical Affirmations of Woman*, p. 171.

5. *Biblical Affirmations of Woman*, p. 171.

6. Herbert's poetry is quoted from *The Works of George Herbert*, ed. F. E. Hutchinson (Oxford: Clarendon Press, 1941).

·12·

God as Female Beloved

Hierarchical assumptions picked up from the patriarchal culture in which we live have blinded our eyes to many things in the Bible. None of these is more important than the liberating news that as the Body of Christ, those who believe actually become "partakers of the divine nature" (II Peter 1:4). Because we are so accustomed to vertical chains of command within pyramid-type power structures, we Christians have been unable to comprehend that Jesus' prayer could actually come true for us: "that they may be one, even as we are one: I in them, and thou in me, that they may be made perfect in one: and that the world may know that thou hast sent me, and hast loved them, as thou hast loved me" (John 17:22–23).

We have been too timid to claim the organic divine-human union that many Scriptures promise us. We are the branches on the vine called Christ. We are the water flowing out of the fountainhead called Christ. We are the church body that is organically connected to the head called Christ. Not only that, but Christ the head is also fully identified with the body: "We are members of [Christ's] body, of [Christ's] flesh and of [Christ's] bones" (Ephesians 5:30). Furthermore, we are instructed to *grow up into the head* (Ephesians 4:15), a directive that makes mincemeat of the notion that Ephesians 5:23 is intended to teach one-way subordination of female to male.

Since head and body are mutually dependent upon each other, the head-body image depicts organic wholeness and mutuality.

What does all this have to do with images of God as female? This: because we are partakers of the divine nature, the love of God toward us is the equal-partner love of one Person of the divine Triad toward another! God loves God's Self within our deepest Selves. No wonder nothing can separate us from the love of God (Romans 8:35–39). And no wonder equal-partner mutuality is the New Testament model for human relationships, embodying as it does the only appropriate kind of relationship between various manifestations or embodiments of God's being.

When we look at the Song of Solomon from this amazing but perfectly biblical perspective, we are enabled to see that erotic poem as a description of God's love for God's self. Not that the book must be read allegorically: it can be read on a purely literal level, as a poem of human sexuality in all its beauty and passion. But through the centuries people have seen another level of meaning in the poem. Jewish readers have seen it as describing the love between God and Israel, with the king who tries to come between the shepherd and his beloved symbolizing the temptations of this world. Mystics have always interpreted the book as depicting the soul's yearning for the often absent shepherd-lover. Others have read it as a fertility myth, the marriage of the sun to the Mother-Earth goddess. And Christians have seen the Song of Solomon as depicting the love between Christ and the church.

Patriarchy assumes that God is masculine—and indeed masculine in all three persons—so that the church can only be exclusively feminine, subordinate, and "other." As we free ourselves from that assumption, we become able to envision an organic human identity with the divine nature that was previously impossible to think about. The risen

Christ, Jesus of Nazareth in a resurrection body that transcends human limitations, is no longer limited by human
maleness. Instead, the risen Christ becomes One Body with
us all. Christ the Bridegroom is also Christ the Bride, in a
flesh-and-bones identification. For this reason, we should
not speak of the risen Christ exclusively as *He* any more
than we should speak of any other transcendent manifestation of God exclusively as *He*. (Nor should we speak of the
church exclusively as *She*). According to the New Testament, the risen Christ actually becomes the new inner nature of every male *and female* who is willing to let the "old
nature" be crucified with its affections and lusts. Christ *is*
the church; the church *is* Christ.

Approached from this perspective, the Song of Songs is
the story of the love of God's self for God's self. The assertive strength of the female as well as the male lover is thus
an indication of equal-partner relationship within the godhead. In the New Testament, only John 17 gives us any
glimpse into that love relationship: Jesus prays that "the
love wherewith thou hast loved me may be in them, and I
in them." But the Song of Songs spells out the relationship
in all the sacred ravishment of a love that is as strong as
death. The female lover is an independent person who
keeps vineyards (1:6), pastures flocks (1:8), and enjoys absolute equality with her lover. He belongs to her as much
as she belongs to him (2:16, 6:3). Furthermore, "his desire
is for [her] (7:10) as opposed to the Genesis 3:16 judgment
that her desire would be toward her husband, who would
rule over her. In the Song of Songs, sinful, joyless submission/dominance is transformed into mutuality and delight."[1] If we feel a bit shocked at the suggestion that the
beloved woman in the Song of Songs may be an image of
God, perhaps that tells us not only about the strength of
our hierarchical sexism but also about our nervousness
concerning human embodiment and sexuality.

Christ has often been hymned as "the rose of Sharon, and the lily of the valley," but in the Song of Songs (2:1) it is clearly *the woman* who calls herself by those names (see the New English Bible or the Jerusalem Bible, which help to clarify who is speaking and when). Yet as Phyllis Trible comments, even when the identity of the speaker is uncertain, that may create a problem for observers but not for "participants who know that in Eros all voices mingle."[2] So we are on legitimate ground when we read the following passage, and others like it, as descriptions of the Christ's very self in the feminine image of the Beloved Woman: "But my dove is unique,/ mine, unique and perfect./ She is the darling of her mother,/ the favorite of the one who bore her. . . . arising like the dawn, fair as the moon, resplendent as the sun,/terrible as an army with banners" (6:8–10). Because the moon is traditionally female and the sun traditionally male, this imagery is remarkably androgynous. It reminds me of the powerful woman in Revelation 12, a woman clothed with the sun and standing on the moon. She is recognized by Christian exegetes to symbolize the Church,[3] the Beloved of Christ and hence also Christ the Beloved.

In past centuries, those who could not believe that a frankly sensual celebration of human love could properly be included in the Bible insisted upon reading the Song of Solomon as an allegory. An allegory is a story in which the plot exists only to point away from itself to another level of meaning. But it is far wiser to read the book symbolically. A symbol has a fully literal meaning but also points to other levels of meaning. Read symbolically from a Christian perspective, the Song of Solomon literally celebrates romantic equal-partner love and figuratively depicts not only the love between Christ and the church but also the love relationship within the godhead. On every level the relationship is utterly mutual; as Trible points out, in the

Song of Songs "There is no male dominance, no female subordination, and no stereotyping of either sex. . . . Love for the sake of love is [the Book's] message. . . . It is a symphony of eroticism."[4]

We are drawn into the godhead's love-relationship by our organic identification with the Anointed One, the Christ. Opening ourselves to this level of meaning could do wonders for our self-concepts as Christian women and men. It could also cast an especially sacred and healing light upon our sexual impulses. And it could remind us of our responsibility to be embodiments, manifestations, or incarnations of God's love to the world in which we live.

NOTES

1. Phyllis Trible, "Women in the Old Testament," *Interpreter's Dictionary of the Bible*, Supplementary Volume (Nashville: Abingdon, 1976), p. 965.

2. *God and the Rhetoric of Sexuality* (Philadelphia: Fortress Press, 1978), p. 145.

3. See, for instance, *Ellicott's Bible Commentary in One Volume* (Grand Rapids, Michigan: Zondervan Publishing House, 1971), p. 1229. (Ellicott even asks comparison of Revelation 12:1 to Canticles 6:10).

4. Trible, *God and the Rhetoric of Sexuality*, pp. 161–162.

·13·

God Our Ezer

The creation account in Genesis 2 depicts God's concern for Adam, the earth creature who is alone in the garden. "I will make [this one] a help meet for him," says God, who promptly creates the beasts and the fowl and brings them to Adam for naming; "but for Adam there was not found a help meet for him." Finally God puts the earth creature into a deep sleep, and from the side of the creature draws out the human female, in relationship with whom Adam becomes a human male.[1] Because the female is a "help meet" for the male, the male is expected to transcend every former relationship life may have offered in order to cherish this "one flesh" relationship.

As most biblical feminists know, the Hebrew words for "help meet" are *ezer neged*, meaning something like "an assistance suitable to" or "appropriate for" the one helped. Hence the focus of the passage is on the uniqueness of human relating, a type of relating that cannot be shared with animals, fish, or birds, no matter how dear to us our pets may be.

Many of us have heard patriarchal interpretations that reduce *ezer neged* to "helpmate," as if the female is mated to the male only in order to serve in a secondary and supportive role as man's helper. But *neged* does not emphasize matedness; rather, it emphasizes appropriateness or suitability, and thus implies equality. And the powerful associations of the word *ezer*, picked up from the way the word is utilized elsewhere, deny any subordinationistic intent in the Genesis narrator's use of the word.

Ezer is used twenty-one times in the Hebrew Scriptures. Three times it refers to vital human assistance in moments of extreme need; sixteen times it speaks of God's direct assistance to human beings; and twice it is applied specifically to Eve, the human female.

Obviously, a word that is used sixteen times concerning divine action is an exalting and glorious word that carries no connotations of secondariness. Even more important is the fact that the Bible applies the word *ezer* to only two specifically named entities: God and Eve. Apparently woman is in some unique sense the channel of God's *ezer* to the world; and conversely, God also is the *ezer* of humankind. If the fact that woman is man's *ezer* carries connotations of servanthood, it is not humiliating slavery but rather service from the vantage point of authentic, innerpowered choice: the kind of servanthood the Creator assumes toward Her/His creatures. It is not that God is at our beck and call to interfere with natural cause-and-effect in our behalf, but instead that by being in touch with Christ the Center and Source of our being, we and God mutually love and empower each other. The analogy with marriage is clear enough, and was made specific by Paul in Ephesians 5.

Speaking of the overused image of God as Father, Linda Clark points out that "there is an interaction between the two terms in a metaphor. Therefore the qualification of meaning applies from fathers to God *and from God to fathers.* There is a change of meaning taking place *in both directions.* . . . God is fatherlike and *fathers are godlike.*"[2] Fortunately, by reclaiming the biblical images of God as female, we can make that process work *for* women as it has worked *against* us through all the centuries of patriarchy.

The fact that the Bible uses the word *ezer* for both Eve and God creates an important analogy: Eve is to Adam as God is to humankind. Eve is Adam's *ezer;* God is humanity's *ezer*. As we open ourselves to it, the metaphor will indeed interact in both directions. If God is *ezer*like, then being man's *ezer* is godlike!

A few passages concerning God as *ezer* may cause the interaction to cast new light on woman's destiny as man's *ezer*. At the same time they may cast new light on our concept of what God is like. For instance, in Exodus 18:4 we are told that the name Eliezer means "My God is an help [an *ezer*]." Specifically, the *ezer* in this case involved deliverance from the sword of Pharoah. Deuteronomy 33:26 (KJV) speaks of "the God of Jesurun, who rideth upon the heaven in thy help [*ezer*]." The Jerusalem Bible makes the point clearer: God "rides the heavens to your rescue." Psalm 70:5 expresses a prayer: "But I am poor and needy; make haste unto me, O God: thou art my help [*ezer*] and my deliverer; O Lord, make no tarrying." And Hosea 13:9 depicts God as saying, "O Israel, thou hast destroyed thyself, but in me is thine help [*ezer*]."

In these absolutely typical passages, the *ezer* is the one who is strong and autonomous, who willingly chooses to come to the aid of the one who is weak and in need. And of course that is exactly the concept of servanthood taught by Jesus and depicted in the Christian Scriptures. Power is not to be used to aggrandize the already powerful, but to empower others. "Whosoever will be chief among you," said Jesus, "let [that one] be your servant" (Matthew 20:27).

One of the traditionalist arguments against mutual submission in marriage is that wives must be one-way submissive to their husbands in order to demonstrate the proper relationship of humankind to God. I have been asked in triumphant tones of "I've got you now!" whether, since I believe husbands should serve wives in mutuality, I also believe that God should serve human beings. To my questioner's obvious disappointment, my answer is yes, indeed, that the Bible teaches not only male-female mutual submission, but also divine-human mutual submission. God's appointing of Adam and Eve as the caretakers of the world and cocreators of society (Genesis 1:26–28) was surely an act of submission on God's part, an act by which God voluntarily stepped back and limited God's self, becoming dependent upon his/her own creatures.

One of the direct results of sexism is that it blinds us to the humble nearness of God, the internal presence of God who is our *ezer*, our servant as well as our master. The Virgin Mary understood the servanthood of God when she sang, "[God] who is mighty has done great things for me ... [God] has put down the mighty from their thrones, and exalted those of low degree; [God] has filled the hungry with good things.... [God] has helped [God's] servant Israel" (Luke 1:49–54, RSV). Here Mary depicts God as the cook and waiter who feeds the hungry, and gives us a perfect description of divine-human mutuality when she tells us that God has served God's own servant.

The Gospels are full of stories about Jesus' pouring out energy on behalf of those who sought his help, and serving his own disciples. The apostle Paul also expressed the servanthood of God by speaking of the Spirit who "helpeth our infirmities" (Romans 8:26). Colossians 1:17 renders God's service cosmic by telling us that Christ holds everything together. And Jesus imaged God as the servant of humanity in John 15:1 (RSV): "I am the true vine, and my Father is the vinedresser." As Geoffrey Hoyland says, "We belong to God and [God] belongs to us; we give ourselves to [God] and [God] gives [Godself] to us, there are no 'ifs' or 'buts' about it."[3] Therefore, by living in respectful mutuality with other human beings, we act out the biblical relationship between creature and Creator.

Through Eve, women are identified as the *ezer* of the

male half of the human race. Directly created by God who is our *ezer* both in huge public matters and in smaller internal crises, womankind is a unique channel of God's power to the world. Julian of Norwich was blunt enough to identify motherhood with God in her book about divine love: "To the property of motherhood belong nature, wisdom and knowledge, and *this is God*."[4] I will follow Dame Julian's example by being blunt and unequivocal: because God is *ezer*like—because God is womanlike—women are Godlike.[5]

NOTES

1. See Phyllis Trible, *God and the Rhetoric of Sexuality* (Philadelphia: Fortress Press, 1978), pp. 72–143.

2. *Image-Breaking/Image-Building*, ed. Linda Clark, Marian Ronan, and Eleanor Walker (New York: Pilgrim Press, 1981), p. 84, emphasis mine.

3. *The Use of Silence* (London: S.P.C.K., 1955), p. 17.

4. *Showings*, trans. Edmund Colledge, O.S.A. and James Walsh, S.J. (New York: Paulist Press, 1978), p. 299, emphasis mine.

5. The male God-imagery in the Bible has been implying all along that *men* are Godlike, and thus empowering men to take responsibility for society. The statement that *women* are Godlike is therefore not an attempt to outdo men, but simply to right the human balance. Naturally, the images of God as female would have to be used frequently in church liturgies, hymns, and sermons, in order for them to have a truly empowering effect on women in society.

·14·

Bakerwoman God

Matthew 13:33 records that Jesus said, "The kingdom[1] of heaven is like the yeast a woman took and
mixed in with three measures of flour till it was leavened all
through." Luke 13:20–21 applies the same image to the
kingdom of God: "What shall I compare the kingdom of
God with? It is like the yeast a woman took and mixed
in with three measures of flour till it was leavened all
through."

Some scholars claim that the leaven is a symbol of corruption and unsound doctrine, so that the woman would be
a false prophet or a demonic figure. In fact, I remember
hearing a sermon on this parable when I was very young.
The preacher explained the point of the parable as this:
when women assume spiritual leadership, the result is always heresy. As a result of such interpretations, we girls
and women sat silently under our hats, waiting for the
Holy Spirit to lead some male to speak, knowing that if we
were to stand up publicly and claim the Spirit's guidance
for ourselves, we would be shown to the door!

There are several reasons why certain scholars interpret
this little story negatively. First, leaven is always a negative
symbol elsewhere in Scripture—hence the requirement of
unleavened bread at Passover. Matthew 16:11 uses leaven
for the false teaching of the Sadducees and Pharisees, while
1 Corinthians 5:6–8 applies the word to moral irresponsi-

bility. Secondly, several of the stories in Matthew 13 indicate that evil *can* infiltrate the kingdom of heaven: the tares are planted in the field of wheat, and bad fish are caught in the dragnet along with the good.

However, there is clear evidence that in the case of this particular parable, the leaven is a positive symbol and the bakerwoman is an image of God. For one thing, there is a major difference between this parable and the ones concerning the wheat field and the dragnet. In both of those parables, Jesus introduced a positive symbol first, then showed that corruption can infiltrate: "The Kingdom of heaven may be compared *to a man who sowed good seed* in his field" (Matt. 13:24) and "The kingdom of heaven is *like a dragnet* cast into the sea that brings in a haul of all kinds" (Matt. 13:47). But in Matt. 13:33, Jesus directly compares the kingdom of heaven to the yeast itself: "The kingdom of heaven is *like the yeast.*" No negative image follows.

Furthermore, the parable of the leaven is distinguished from the two parables that introduce corruption into the kingdom of heaven by being utilized as a parable concerning the kingdom of *God* in Luke 13. Neither the dragnet nor the wheat/tares parable appears in Luke 13, where only the mustard seed and the yeast are similitudes to clarify the nature of God's kingdom.

Why did Jesus use yeast in a positive sense in this parable, when he himself had warned against the yeast of the Pharisees and Sadducees? Apparently Jesus was thinking in each case of the peculiar action of yeast in flour—a kind of putrescence or fermentation that changes the nature of the flour for either good or evil, depending on one's point of view. Jesus apparently was familiar with the female job of baking bread, and while he knew the traditional Jewish attitude toward leaven, he must have sufficiently enjoyed bread that had been raised to see yeast also as a positive influence. Just as the yeast permeates the three measures of meal and causes them to puff up, so a good influence can permeate all the opinions and actions of a society. Harrell F. Beck of Boston University School of Theology puts it this way: " 'Leaven' is used in a good sense in the parable of the leaven (Matthew 13:33, Luke 13:20–21), in which Jesus likens the silent, unrelenting growth of the kingdom of God among [humankind] to the pervasive assimilating action of the yeast."[2]

What gives us the right to see the woman as an image of God herself? The answer lies in the parallelism of the parables of the kingdom in Matthew 13. Who sows good wheat, and when the enemy sows tares, gives orders that the wheat and tares should grow together until the harvest? Who sows the tiny mustard seed? Who is the treasure in the field? The pearl of great price? The owner of the drag-net whose fishers divide the good fish from the bad? Jesus helps us answer these questions by interpreting two of the parables for us. The angels of God will divide the wicked from the just, explains Jesus about the fish in the dragnet; and as for the field, "the sower of the good seed is the Son of Man" (i.e., Christ, The Human One). By the principle of parallelism, then, the woman who puts yeast into her three measures of meal is also an image of God's action. So we have here yet another instance of Jesus' depicting divine nature in female terms. In first-century culture, had Jesus done that only once, that one instance would have been extraordinary. The fact that he did it repeatedly strongly drives home the point of human equality.

Jesus also used a female-associated image when he called himself the living bread, the bread of life, the bread from heaven (John 6:31–35). If God provided the manna from heaven for Israel in the wilderness, then God is being compared to a heavenly baker—and *women* did the baking in the ancient Hebrew culture. If Jesus is "the bread of God . . . which comes down from heaven," then God is the baker of the bread—and *women* did the baking in first-century Palestine.

Alla Bozarth-Campbell has captured the personal application of this beautiful God-image in the first stanza of her poem "Bakerwoman God."

> Bakerwoman God,
> I am your living bread.
> Strong, brown, Bakerwoman God,
> I am your low, soft, and being-
> shaped loaf.
> I am your rising
> bread, well-kneaded
> by some divine and knotty
> pair of knuckles, by your warm earth-hands.
> I am bread well-kneaded.[3]

As Christ is, so are we in this world—the living bread prepared by the divine Bakerwoman.

NOTES

1. I do not find *Kingdom* a particularly relevant image for modern Americans, nor are its masculine and classist associations helpful. However, in order to be as clear as possible about the biblical basis for the image of God as Bakerwoman, I have decided to leave *Kingdom* as is in this chapter. For lectionary usage and in my own speaking, I prefer to use words such as *commonwealth, sphere,* or *realm.*

2. "Leaven," *The Interpreter's Dictionary of the Bible* (Nashville: Abingdon Press, 1962), Volume III, pp. 104–105.

3. The entire poem is reprinted in Linda Clark, Marian Ronan, and Eleanor Walker, *Image-Breaking/Image-Building* (New York: The Pilgrim Press, 1981), pp. 70–71. Originally published in *In God's Image: Toward Wholeness for Women and Men,* ed. La Vonne Althouse and Lois K. Snook (New York: Division for Mission in North America, Lutheran Church in America, 1976), p. 13.

·15·

God as Mother Eagle

There are two types of wing-images in the Bible. In one type, a human being images herself (or himself) snuggled safely *under* God's sheltering wings. In the other type, a human being images himself (or herself) being lifted up upon divine wings. I think I can demonstrate that both of these wing-images are depicting God as female. As we will see in the next chapter, the under-the-wing-images are predominantly images of God as Mother Hen, although there is nothing to stop us from substituting a nesting dove or even a nesting eagle or other bird in most passages where this image appears. By contrast, the on-the-wing images are depictions of God as Mother Eagle.

Speaking of Jacob as representing Yahweh's people, Deuteronomy 32:11–12 (KJV) says, "As an eagle stirreth up her nest, fluttereth over her young, spreadeth abroad her wings, taketh them, beareth them on her wings: so the Lord alone did lead Jacob. . . ." Similarly, Exodus 19:4 pictures God as telling the children of Israel, "I bare you on eagles' wings, and brought you unto myself." And in Job 39:27–30 Yahweh asks Job from the whirlwind, "Doth the eagle mount up at thy command, and make her nest on high?" Clearly the unspoken answer to this rhetorical question is that the female eagle is an expression of the will not of Job, but of God; and Deuteronomy and Exodus depict the female eagle not simply as behaving according to

God's will, but as actually *imaging the nature of God in relationship to her children.*

Whereas traditional imagery often depicts God as masculine and the children of God as feminine in relationship to him, the eagle imagery reverses that equation, as do all the images of God as female. God is the mother eagle, and we human beings are the eaglets learning to be self-sustaining (Job 39 goes on to imply the process of the mother eagles' teaching the eaglets to hunt). When the sex of the young eagles is suggested or specified, it seems to be masculine, as in the parallelism of Isaiah 40:31–32: "Even the youths shall faint and be weary, and the young men shall utterly fall: but they that wait upon the Lord shall renew their strength; they shall mount up with wings as eagles. . . ."[1]

The biblical image of God-as-feminine-eagle and humanity-as-masculine- or non-sex-specific-eaglets is especially important because as I have mentioned earlier, certain Christians insist on wifely submission on the basis that the Bible depicts humanity as feminine in relationship to a masculine God. I have repeatedly heard statements to the effect that if a wife fails to obey her husband, her example tends to erode human awareness of proper creaturely submission to the Creator. This idolatry of the male is thinly veiled by pointing to biblical images of God as Father and Husband. But even if there were no other images of God as female than the ones of the mother eagle, they alone should be enough to explode the notion that it was God's intention for one sex to be subordinate to another because of a divine-human parallel. Furthermore, the mother eagle images depict a God who is *actively trying to create equals by empowering the eaglets* to take care of themselves. Hence these images do not encourage dominance and submission *even in our relationship with the Creator*, let alone our relationships with other human beings!

Deuteronomy 32 and Job 39 seem to depict the mother eagle teaching her eaglets to fly and to hunt their own food. I have been told that the mother eagle takes the eaglets on her wings, swoops downward suddenly to force them into solo flight, then stays close to swoop under them again whenever they grow too weary to continue on their own. What a picture of a loving God, caring nurturantly for us when we are weak, yet always aiming at the goal of our maturity and internalized strength rather than at morbid dependency upon a force external to ourselves!

Several years ago I had a memorable dream of an eagle. It was sitting inside a huge circus tent or building, on a post or piling that stood just above my eye level. From this perch the eagle gazed down into my eyes with the most infinite, amused, tender love imaginable. The next day I consulted my books on dreams and symbols and was told that because eagles are identified with the sun and with male fertilization, with high flight and with speed, they symbolize the Father, Divine Majesty, domination, and heroism. Dante, I was reminded, calls the eagle "the bird of God."

While I was glad to be dreaming of God's tenderness toward me, still as a feminist I felt discouraged that my unconscious mind was handing up masculine God symbols. The dream seemed a warning that my deep mind continued to be very sexist. Of course I was viewing eagles only as they were filtered through the interpretative grid provided by my symbol books and commentaries. For that reason I did not even notice that the Bible several times depicted God as a *female* eagle.

Since the only Bible used in the church of my youth was a King James Version, I really should have noticed the images of God as Mother Eagle. They were not at all obscured by the translation I was reading—only by my own well groomed expectations. But several other translations of Deuteronomy 32:11–12 will demonstrate how the art of

translation can make a female God-image disappear. The
Jerusalem Bible reads, "Like an eagle watching over its
nest,/ hovering over its young,/ he spreads out his wings to
hold him/ he supports him on his pinions." People hearing
this passage read aloud are barraged by six male pronouns
in two brief lines of poetry, and the eagle becomes either
neuter (*its*) or male (*his*). Since in point of fact the female
eagle does far more of the incubation of the eggs than the
male eagle, and far more of the hunting (except during the
first few days when she must tear up the meat killed by the
male for the newborn eaglets), and since she is both larger
and stronger than the male eagle,[2] the King James translators were just and right to utilize female pronouns to specify that Deuteronomy speaks of God as a *female* eagle. By
contrast the Jerusalem Bible translators have made the divine mother eagle vanish into a patriarchal confusion. The
New English Bible does the same thing, as does the Re-
vised Standard Version. No wonder the eagle image has
seemed to many readers to be masculine!

In case we need further authorization to associate the
Bible's eagle imagery with the female, Revelation 12 provides it. Whereas the middle portion of the chapter uses the
image of a war in heaven, the first and final portions depict
the triumph of a woman and the seed of the woman
through purely nonviolent means. Among these pacifistic
methods we find that "she was given a huge pair of eagle's
wings to fly away from the serpent into the desert"; and
thus the serpent's desire to destroy her is defeated.

Since women are relatively rarely the focus of Scripture,
it is vital to pay attention to what happens in Revelation 12.
The divine purpose is centered upon a woman who not
only gives birth to the divine—her child is immediately
snatched up to God's throne—but also symbolically *herself
assumes divinity* by flying with the wings of a great eagle.
This powerful woman, clothed with the sun and standing

upon the moon, has traditionally been identified with the church, those believers who have by faith become identified with Christ, the firstborn of the New Humanity. Charles John Ellicott rightly connects the woman's eagle wings with the wings of Exodus 19:4 and Deuteronomy 32:10–12,[3] though he fails to specify that all of these images are of God as *female* eagle. What happens in Revelation 12 is that a female church is divinized so that she assumes the wings of God the great mother eagle. The process is the one described by "God eternal" to Catherine of Siena: "I, God, became [human] and humanity became God through the union of my divine nature with your human nature. This greatness is given to every person in general...."[4]

The structure of Revelation 12 also shows another process occurring: female, pacifistic triumph over the serpent/dragon encircles male, militaristic imagery. Phyllis Trible has analyzed the lyric poem in Jeremiah 31:15–22, showing that in that lyric, the form as well as the content embodies a womb: "Yahweh has created a new thing in the land: female surrounds man" (Jeremiah 31:22).[5] The same sort of process occurs in Revelation 12. And surely it tells us something about ourselves that in Christian history, the imagery that has received widespread currency is the male-oriented militaristic imagery of Revelation 12:7–12: "Onward Christian Soldiers," "The Battle Hymn of the Republic," "A Mighty Fortress Is Our God," and all the rest. In a world trembling on the brink of nuclear disaster, surely we need to turn away from militaristic imagery and toward the female, nonviolent kinds of images employed in Revelation 12:1–6 and 13–17!

Not every orthodox Christian through the ages has been blind to the fact that the Old Testament images of being carried on God's wings are female images. Adam of Perseigne, a twelfth-century Cistercian abbot, wrote that a bishop's business was to "like an eagle provoking her chicks to fly flutter over them and bear upwards in your wings both by word and example those little ones commended to you."[6] And a contemporary of ours has written a hymn concerning the image, to be sung to the tune of that old gospel song, "Stand Up, Stand Up for Jesus":

OUR GOD IS LIKE AN EAGLE

When Israel camped in Sinai, then Moses heard from
  God.
This message tell the people, and give them this my
  word,
From Egypt I was with you and carried on my wing,
The whole of your great nation from slav'ry I did
  bring.

Just as a mother eagle who helps her young to fly,
I am a mother to you; your needs I will supply.
And you are as my children, my own who hear my
  voice.
I am a mother to you, the people of my choice.

If God is like an eagle who helps her young [be free]
And God is also father, then what of you and [me?]
We have no fear of labels; we have no fear of roles,
If God's own being blends them, we seek the selfsame
  goal.

Our God is not a woman; our God is not a man.
Our God is both and neither; our God is I who am.
From all the roles that bind us, our God has set us
  free.
What freedom does God give us? The freedom just to
  be.[7]

This hymn demonstrates why some people are desperately anxious to deny that the Bible ever compares God to a woman or to any female creature whatsoever. The more a person's energies are invested in maintaining *status quo* concerning male/female socialization and sex roles, the more threatening are the biblical images of God as female. For as the hymn points out, if God's own nature blends the male and female roles, then human beings are also free to develop each of their gifts, without worrying about society's sex role assignments. That this was God's intention is supported by many factors in the Bible: the assignment of care for all creation to both male and female in Genesis 1, for instance; and the assertion that in Christ sexual barriers are transcended (Galatians 3:28); and the androgynous imagery that calls both females *and males* the bride of Christ, both males *and females* the sons of God.[8]

From another standpoint, as the hymn points out, God is *neither* male *nor* female. The biblical images of God as female, standing like a sort of "minority report" next to the predominantly male God-imagery, will help to keep us reminded of that fact. The Judeo-Christian habit of using almost exclusively masculine references to God, with exclusively masculine pronouns, has drawn us willy-nilly toward idolatry of the male. According to the Bible, our God is *both* male and female, *and neither* male nor female. The language of prayer, liturgy, sermon, and hymnody had best reflect that fact.

Genesis 1:2 tells us that "the Spirit of God moved upon the face of the waters." The word *rachaph*, here translated "moved upon" or "hovered," also means "to shake" and "to flutter." The word is used only three times in the Old Testament, and only twice concerning God's action. The only use of *rachaph* concerning God other than Genesis 1:2 occurs when Deuteronomy 32:11-12 depicts God as the female eagle fluttering over her young. So although the enormous influence of Milton's *Paradise Lost* has taught us to see Genesis 1:2 as a dove image, the similar use of *rachaph* in Genesis and Deuteronomy makes it more probable that *the very first image in the Bible is of God as a mother eagle fluttering over the waters* as she gives birth to the universe.

In Egyptian hieroglyphics, the letter A is represented by the eagle, standing for the Origin of all things and the warmth of life. We are only reclaiming our biblical and cultural heritage when we see that origin not in terms of masculine impregnation, but rather in terms of feminine involvement in the birth and nurturing process. God is our mother-eagle.[9] In her we safely put our trust.

NOTES

1. It would, of course, be absurd to conclude that because this eaglet image is apparently addressed to males, the image excludes females from God's "nest." Males were understood to be the human norm in the Old Testament culture, so the maleness must be interpreted as inclusive of the female.

2. "Falconiformes," *The New Encyclopedia Britannica, Macropaedia* (1979), Volume 7, pp. 145–152; and Griffin Bancroft, *Vanishing Wings: A Tale of Three Birds of Prey* (New York: Franklin Watts, 1972), p. 14.

3. *Ellicott's Bible Commentary in One Volume* (Grand Rapids, Michigan: Zondervan Publishing House, 1971), p. 1230.

4. Catherine of Siena, *The Dialogue*, trans. Suzanne Noffke (New York: Paulist Press, 1980), p. 205.

5. *God and the Rhetoric of Sexuality* (Philadelphia: Fortress Press, 1978), pp. 40–50. See also Leonard Swidler, *Biblical Affirmations of Woman* (Philadelphia: The Westminster Press, 1979), pp. 31–32.

6. Caroline Walker Bynum, *Jesus as Mother* (Berkeley: University of California Press, 1982), p. 125.

7. Words by Laurence G. Bernier, 1974. "Our God Is Like An Eagle" appears in the UFMCC Trial Hymnal, UFMCC, 5300 Santa Monica Blvd., Suite 304, Los Angeles, CA 90029. The Trial Hymnal is available for $4.50. The words in square brackets have been changed by me to correct a grammatical error.

8. For more on the issue of the Bible and sex role socialization, see Letha Scanzoni and Nancy Hardesty, *All We're Meant to Be* (Waco: Word, 1974), and Virginia R. Mollenkott, *Women, Men, and the Bible* (Nashville: Abingdon, 1977).

9. A booklet entitled *As An Eagle: The Holy Spirit Mother* (June 1981), is available from Lois I. Roden, P.O. Box 4098, Waco, Texas 76705. As much as I sympathize with Lois Roden's attempts to prove

that the Holy Spirit is the feminine component of the Holy Trinity (the Father, the Mother, and the Son), I reiterate my belief that we are wiser to stick to the Bible's own usage, which is to associate feminine as well as masculine and neuter imagery with *all three persons* of the Godhead.

·16·

God as Mother Hen

The most obvious and for Christians the controlling use of the Mother Hen image occurs in Matthew 23:27 (and Luke 13:34), where we are told that Jesus lamented, "Jerusalem, Jerusalem, you that kill the prophets and stone those who are sent to you! How often have I longed to gather your children, as a hen gathers her chicks under her wings, and you refused!" The point of this lamentation for us today is of course not that the people of Jerusalem were stubborn and afraid of God's love as Jesus offered it to them, but rather that we ourselves are like the people of Jerusalem. *We* are the people who murder the prophets who bring us jolting insights—not with execution, in most cases, but rather with nasty gossip and official ostracizing and personal rejection. And *we* are the people who refuse to let the child within us cuddle inside the safety of God's protective wings. Because we have a deep-seated fear of being known and loved to the uttermost, we discover ourselves to be (all too often) the chicks who *will not be gathered.*

The difference between God-as-hen and God-as-eagle is the difference between intimate cuddling and dynamic empowerment. We need both. Sometimes feminists especially are so determined to overcome societal conditioning by becoming self-sustaining and autonomous that we try to repress the little child inside, the baby who cries out for nurturance. But the child will not be denied without causing serious damage to our inner being. The same God who as mother eagle shoves us out of the nest and teaches us to fly and feed ourselves is also, at other times, the mother hen clucking for us to relax within the security of her loving wings.

Viewed from another angle, the magnificent eagle images are associated with light, with the sun, with height and mobility and exteriority, while the lowly hen images are associated with the shadows and darkness of the henhouse, and with depth and stillness and interiority beneath the mothering wings. Again, we need both. Women especially are afraid to face the anger, the self hatred, the fears, the masochism, the hostilities—all the things we Christian women were never supposed to feel. Many men need to get in touch with the weaknesses and vulnerabilities that are tied to their nurturant capacities and strengths—all those things men were not supposed to feel. In the protected environment of God's unconditional love, we can come to terms with our shadow-selves.

When Jesus used the image of the hen and her chicks, he was speaking from the point of view of a being outside of human history (that is, speaking as God's Wisdom), and was expressing unconditional love toward those who were in the process of rejecting him and that eternal One who sent him.[1] Such love, realized and internalized, provides the secure matrix within which we can begin to confront our "negative" or "unacceptable" traits and incorporate them creatively into our personalities.

Jesus no doubt knew that when he compared himself to a mother hen, he was tapping into, making explicit, a well-established image from the Hebrew Scriptures. Certainly the author of II Esdras, an apocryphal book dating from the first century C.E., understood Jesus' hen image as tapping into a Hebrew understanding of God as both father and mother and internal authentic Self. II Esdras 1:27–30 (KJV) reads, "You have not as it were forsaken me, but your own selves, saith the Lord. Thus says the Almighty Lord, Have I not prayed you as a father his sons, as a mother her daughters, and a nurse her young babes, That ye would be my people, and I would be your God; that ye would be my children, and I should be your father? I gathered you together, as a hen gathers her chickens under her wings." The alternation of male and female God-images in this context of psychological health suggests that the author intuited a connection between psychological empowerment and being able to identify with an image of God as being the same sex as oneself. (Notice that the father speaks to the sons; the mother to the daughters.)

Jesus also had plenty of canonical precedent for his mother-hen image. For instance, in the ancient book of Ruth, when Boaz praised Ruth for her care of Naomi, he said, "May the Lord recompense you for what you have done, and a full reward be given you by the Lord, the God of Israel, *under whose wings you have come to take refuge* (Ruth 2:12, Oxford RSV, emphasis mine). Later, Ruth takes Boaz up on that blessing, urging him to "spread your wing [*Kānāp*, the same word used in 2:12] over your maidservant, for you are a redeemer."[2] Sometimes the shelter of God's wing is supplied through human embodiment! Ruth calls Boaz to take responsibility *to bring about the good wishes he has showered upon her.*

Whereas the eagle images speak of being *stirred up by* or *carried upon* the wings of God, the hen images speak of warmth and protection *under* God's wings. The Psalms frequently speak of this aspect of God's motherhood: "From those who revolt against you/ guard me like the pupil of your eye;/ hide me in the shadow of your wings/ from the onslaughts of the wicked" (17:8–9). Psalm 57 begins with this plea: "Take pity on me, God, take pity on me, in you my soul takes shelter; / I take shelter in the shadow of your wings / until the destroying storm is over." Psalm 61:4 prays for everlasting protection: "Let me stay in your tent for ever, / taking refuge in the shelter of your wings." And Psalm 91:4 promises that those who are able to trust God's love will be covered by God's feathers and will find shelter underneath God's wings. So when Jesus spoke of his yearning to be like a protective mother hen toward the people of Jerusalem, he was identifying his mission with the divine compassion that permeates so much of Scripture. As we saw earlier, the Hebrew word for God's compassion could accurately be translated *womb-love.*

St. Anselm, archbishop of Canterbury from 1093 until his death in 1109, clearly grasped the implications of Jesus' hen-image, for he wrote, "But you, Jesus, good lord, are you not also a mother? Are you not that mother who, like a hen, collects her chickens under her wings? Truly, master, you are a mother. For what others have conceived and given birth to, they have received from you. . . . You are the author, others are the ministers. It is then you, above all, Lord God, who are mother." And he urges his own soul to "run under the wings of your mother Jesus and bewail your sorrows. . . ."[3] It is interesting that Anselm uses a *double* mother image here: Christ's *ministers* are mothers; they are able to conceive and give birth because their *master* is also a mother—the mother "above all." The whole concept of women's ordination looks different from Anselm's perspective. If Christ's ministers are mothers because of the motherhood of Jesus, what possible problem should we have with ordaining women to the priesthood or ministry?

Other Christians who have used the sheltering wing image in a female context include William of St. Thierry and Adam, abbot of Perseigne. Adam uses the image to reprimand a bishop who is failing to be tender enough toward those in his charge: "In what way are you yourself named father or mother of little ones, you who do not jealously watch over your chicks with tender affection as a hen does ... ?" To Adam, a good father must always be also a good mother.[4] Again, from our perspective Adam's words imply that a healthy priesthood would include women as well as men. For after all, most males tend to undervalue their own feminine component when society regards as secondary the personhood of real women.

But the primary significance of the image of God as mother hen probably remains personal and inward. God's love for us is so sheltering and unconditional that we need not fear to face either ourselves or others. If we can trust the words of Boaz to Ruth and the wing-images of the Psalmist, the same Person whom Jesus called Father was, like Jesus, a reliably protective mother hen as well.

NOTES

1. Although there is anger in what Jesus says immediately thereafter: "So be it! Your house will be left to you desolate," there is also the promise of redemption, for desolation will end when the people say, "Blessings on [the one] who comes in the name of the Lord!" (Matthew 23:39; cf. Psalm 118:26). The love is free for the taking.

2. Phyllis Trible, *God and the Rhetoric of Sexuality* (Philadelphia: Fortress Press, 1978), p. 184.

3. Caroline Walker Bynum, *Jesus as Mother* (Berkeley: University of California Press, 1982), p. 114. The Anselm quotation was first pointed out to me by Jane Wilcox, diaconal minister at Mt. Vernon United Methodist Church in Wichita, Kansas.

4. Bynum, pp. 119–120 and pp. 124–125.

·17·

God as Dame Wisdom

Lady Wisdom is the one biblical depiction of God as female that is almost always noticed by scholarly commentators, although the significance of her being *female* is not discussed. For instance, James L. Crenshaw of Vanderbilt University speaks of the Bible's giving voice to "a tradition about Lady Wisdom" who becomes "an expression of divine personality."[1] And Hans G. Conzelmann of the University of Göttingen stresses that "The God of the Christian faith is no other than the God of the wisdom of Israel, the one God, the creator. . . . Wisdom thus serves as an element of continuity from the Old Testament and Judaism to earliest Christianity."[2] That the centrally important figure of Wisdom is *female* is of no particular interest to either of these scholars.

Nevertheless, Dame Wisdom is the image of God as female used most often by biblical authors, appearing frequently in the canonical Book of Proverbs and also in the deuterocanonical books of Wisdom of Solomon, Baruch, and Ecclesiasticus. (Roman Catholics and Eastern Orthodox people accept these latter books as part of the Bible, while Judaism and Protestantism place them outside of the canonical Bible, in the Apocrypha.) Wisdom is also discussed at length in the twenty-eighth chapter of Job; but in that chapter wisdom is not personified, simply being identified as "the fear of the Lord."

Proverbs 1:20–33 depicts Wisdom (*Hokmah*) as crying aloud at street corners, raising her voice in the public squares, offering her saving counsel to anybody who will listen to her. Wisdom's behavior runs directly counter to the socialization of a proper lady, who is taught to be rarely seen and even more rarely heard in the sphere of public activity. Assertive, insistent, and noisy: according to modern definition, Wisdom is a woman but no lady!

Wisdom's anger at being rejected and ignored (Proverbs 1:24–27) is reminiscent of the rejection of God's servant in Isaiah 53:3 and elsewhere. This equation of Dame Wisdom with God's own action in the world is strengthened in the Book of Ecclesiasticus, a Greek translation of an earlier Hebrew work, dating from about 190 B.C.E. Ecclesiasticus 24:3 says that Wisdom came forth from God's mouth to cover the earth like a mist, referring to the incident described in Genesis 2:6, when the mist arose out of the ground to water the earth before rain had been provided. The Wisdom of Solomon, an extraordinarily beautiful book written in Greek during the first century B.C.E., makes explicit the relationship between Wisdom, the mist, and God's creative spirit: "Like a fine mist she [Wisdom] rises from the power of God, a pure effluence from the glory of the Almighty. ..." (7:25, NEB). Just as the mist arose to water the earth before the advent of rain, so Dame Wisdom rises like a mist from God's powerful being in order to enter into holy souls, make them God's friends and prophets (Wisdom 7:25–27), and confer immortality upon them (Wisdom 8:13 and 18).

Ecclesiasticus 24:4 says that Dame Wisdom lives in the pillar of cloud, while Exodus 13:21 and 16:10 make clear that the very presence of God was in that cloud. (As we saw earlier, God's Shekinah glory within the cloud is, like Wisdom, a female depiction of God.) Furthermore, Wisdom 1:5 refers to Wisdom as "the holy spirit of instruction" that "shuns deceit." In the passage immediately following, Wisdom, God, and the spirit of Yahweh are used as synonyms, as interchangeable terms:

> Wisdom is a spirit, a friend to [humankind],
> though she will not pardon the words of a
>   blasphemer,
> since God sees into the innermost parts of him [or her],
> truly observes [the] heart,
> and listens to [the] tongue.
> The spirit of [Yahweh], indeed, fills the whole world,
> and that which holds all things together knows every
>   word that is said (Wisdom 1:6–7).

Clearly, Lady Wisdom is being equated with God, with the Spirit of Yahweh, and with "that which holds all things together." (In Colossians 1:17, *Christ* is identified as the one who "holds all things in unity.") Not only that, but living with Wisdom is specified as absolutely essential to pleasing God (Wisdom 7:28)—implying that unless all of us incorporate the traits Western culture has assigned to women, there is no hope of God's blessing! Wisdom 8:7–8 makes the implication more explicit: temperance, prudence, justice, and fortitude are the fruit of Wisdom's labors, and "nothing in life is more serviceable to [people] than these." The relationship to the New Testament fruits of the Spirit, against which there is no law, should be obvious.

In fact, Wisdom 9:17–18 specifically equates Wisdom with "[God's] holy spirit from above" sent down for the salvation of humankind. Proverbs gives canonical support to all of this, picturing Wisdom as the first thing everyone should acquire (4:7), as the giver of life (4:22 and 7:2), and as the mistress of discretion, lucidity, sound judgment, perception, and justice (8:12–15).

Not only is Dame Wisdom treated as synonymous with

God, with the Old Testament spirit of Yahweh, and with the New Testament Holy Spirit; she is also pictured in terms that link her to Jesus the Christ, the Logos, the Word of God. Wisdom is frequently linked with God's act of creation (Proverbs 3:19 and 8:27, Psalm 104:24, Psalm 136:5, Wisdom 7:22, and 9:9). The Wisdom of Solomon in fact calls *Lady Wisdom* the designer of everything (8:7), whereas Colossians 1:16 says that *Christ* was the creator of everything. Wisdom 7:26 calls *Wisdom* the image of God's goodness; Colossians 1:15 calls *Christ* the "image of the unseen God."

Furthermore, whereas Proverbs 8:22 identifies *Wisdom* as the first created being, Colossians 1:15 states that *Christ* was the first-born of every creature. And whereas Proverbs 8:27–30 says Wisdom was "a master craftsman" when God made the world and Baruch 3:32 depicts Wisdom's presence with God as God created in the beginning, John 1:1 also specifies that the Logos or word was with God in the beginning. Conzelmann says that "as a hypostasis, Logos is analogous to Sophia [Wisdom] . . . the historical person Jesus is proclaimed as the cosmic Logos. . . . This is a christological transformation of wisdom."[3]

St. Augustine directly identified Jesus with Wisdom by means of a previously discussed biblical image, God as mother hen:

> Let us put our egg under the wings of that Hen
> of the Gospel, which crieth out to that false and
> abandoned city, "O Jerusalem, Jerusalem, how
> often would I have gathered thy children together,
> even as a hen her chickens, and thou wouldest
> not!" Let it not be said to us, "How often
> would I, and thou wouldest not!" For that hen
> is the Divine Wisdom.[4]

Elsewhere, St. Augustine calls Wisdom "Our Mother,"[5] and it is interesting to see him implying the masculinity of humankind as we "put our egg" under the wings of that female divinity, the "Hen of the Gospel," Divine Wisdom.

According to Proverbs, *Wisdom* is the path, the knowledge, the way that ensures life (4:11, 22, 26), just as to John *Christ* is the way, the truth, and the life (14:6). Like Christ, Wisdom lives at the side of God, is God's "darling," and delights in humankind (Proverbs 8:30-31, Wisdom 8:3 and 9, Wisdom 9:4 and 10).[6] Like Christ, Wisdom is the Word of God (Ecclesiasticus 24:3, Wisdom 9:1-2). Like Christ, Wisdom makes all things new (Wisdom 7:27). Like Christ, Wisdom is "a reflection of the eternal light,/ untarnished mirror of God's active power,/ image of [God's] goodness" (7:26; cf. Hebrews 1:3).

No wonder Jesus is called the wisdom of God (Luke 11:49 and I Corinthians 1:24)! Even when the reference is very obviously to Jesus in human form, wisdom preserves her feminine gender: "The Son of Man came, eating and drinking, and they say, 'Look, a glutton and a drunkard, a friend of tax collectors and sinners.' Yet wisdom has been proved right by her actions" (Matthew 11:19). As Conzelmann recognizes, Jesus is here "ultimately identified ... with hypostatized wisdom."[7] All of this would seem to indicate that by thinking of the Christ in exclusively masculine terms, we have been ignoring some very important symbols that the earthly Jesus embodied—not only deity and humanity, not only time and eternity, but also masculine and feminine.

Ann Belford Ulanov has written that "the paucity of feminine symbolism in the Godhead of Protestantism and Judaism contribute to the estrangement of Protestant and Jewish women from their own deeper natures."[8] I might add that although the condition of Catholic women is alleviated by veneration of the Virgin Mary, she cannot provide a healthy role model for ordinary women because none of us can be both virgin and mother simultaneously (unless perhaps we live celibate and give birth spiritually).

And in the past Mary's character has been misinterpreted as a "feminine" (even masochistic) passivity engaged in one-way submission to an exclusively masculine God. So Catholic as well as Protestant and Jewish women need a new look at the dynamic, assertive character of Mary the Mother of Jesus, who was so like Wisdom in her loving power. Désirée Hirst in fact connects Mary with Wisdom in a very astute comment: "The figure of Mary evokes something beyond her own nature, or role, however perfect. Like the Wisdom figure of the deuterocanonical books of the Bible, she mirrors the Divine Nature Itself, especially in its most hidden and profound facet . . . that Motherhood which is the complement of the Fatherhood of God. . . ."[9] So indeed do all the other Biblical images of God as female.

Toni Wolff has written, "The image of God is the supreme symbol of the highest human attributes and of the most far-reaching ideas of the human spirit. How then can a woman find herself if her own psychological principle and all its complexities are not objectified in a symbol. . . . The symbol takes effect in the human being by gradually unfolding its meaning."[10] Dame Wisdom is an especially important symbol for contemporary women because she gets us beyond the concept that femaleness finds its primary fulfilment in motherhood. Wisdom is busy in the public sphere; she is no shrinking violet, no vessel waiting to be given her significance by someone else.

Wisdom's actions remind us that when a well-meaning woman praised Jesus' mother for her biological functions—"Happy the womb that bore you and the breasts you sucked!"—Jesus replied, "Still happier are those who hear the word of God and keep it!" (Luke 11:27–28). Jesus was certainly not downing either motherhood or his own mother; he was pointing out that the focus should not be on the *vehicle* by which Mary did the will of God but rather on the *tenor* of her attitudes and her actions. For *some* women, hearing God's word and doing it may involve physical motherhood; and for *all* of us (male and female) there will be the spiritual motherhood of giving birth to ourselves and receiving the Christ-nature into ourselves. But Wisdom crying in the streets reminds us that motherhood is not the be-all and end-all of our existence in this world. Yahweh loves justice (Isaiah 61:8), and it is through Wisdom that "the great impose justice on the world" (Proverbs 8:16).

Wisdom cries out the principle of mutuality: "I love those who love me / . . . I walk in the way of virtue / in the paths of justice, / enriching those who love me, / filling their treasuries" (Proverbs 8:17 and 20–21). This principle of mutuality is particularly important to combat faulty female socialization that defines a good woman as continually superhumanly giving of herself in the support of others. Women must learn to support first themselves, not simply for selfish reasons but also for the sake of others, since other people only tend to become weaker when they are overwhelmed with constant supportiveness. Wisdom's insistence on the *returns* of love, on a *two-way* flow of energy, is important for those of us who need to learn to restrain ourselves from giving too much of ourselves.[11]

Our culture implies that some people must be losers so that others can be winners—and women, black people, native Americans, Hispanics, and other minority persons have been trained to be the all-forgiving everlasting losers. But the Bible teaches a mutuality in which everyone wins because the strong, by empowering others, bless themselves. To those with power in society Christ taught that giving is receiving, that forgiving is to be forgiven, that to free is to be free (Luke 6:37–38). The psychological principle is not one of masochistic sacrifice but of spiritual gaining through spiritual giving, Wisdom's "enriching those who love" her.

As one person in Christ, everybody in the New Humanity either wins together or loses together. In the New Creation we are all guiltless members of One Body, so we can afford to respond to each other with love rather than with fear, all the while maintaining a critical balance by which we do not overextend ourselves. Instead of repressing guilt and then projecting it onto other persons or groups, we are encouraged by the example of Holy Lady Wisdom to reinforce our own sense of acceptability by affirming others as holy and acceptable.

It is self-destructive to wrong those who are One Body with us; so no attempts to subordinate each other can be meaningful to mature members of the New Age, the New Humanity (cf. Romans 13:8–10). Although some rightwing Christians have tried to define a concern for social justice as mere secularism, we have seen that the Bible equates justice with Wisdom and Wisdom with the Christ. So in our minds there can be no division between individual, privatized righteousness and the attempt to correct the societal, structural forms of justice.

In the Hebrew Scriptures, personal and social renewal was accomplished by Holy Lady Wisdom; in the Christian Scriptures, it is Lord Christ who makes all things new. The combination of Wisdom/Christ leads to a healthy blend of male and female imagery that empowers everyone and works beautifully to symbolize the One God who is neither male nor female and yet both male and female. In such a God we have a "supreme symbol of the highest human attributes." Letting this symbol unfold within us, we can live with less fear and therefore more love. As twice-born members of the New Humanity, we are "in Christ Jesus, who of God is made unto us wisdom"(I Corinthians 1:30 KJV).

NOTES

1. "Wisdom in the Old Testament," *Interpreter's Dictionary of the Bible*, Supplementary Volume (Nashville: Abingdon, 1976), p. 956.

Crenshaw says Lady Wisdom is "strongly reminiscent of extrabiblical models, Maat and Ishtar."

2. "Wisdom in the New Testament," *Interpreter's Dictionary of the Bible,* Supplementary Volume, p. 958. In *Biblical Affirmations of Woman,* Leonard Swidler quotes Conzelmann as saying that "Personified Wisdom's . . . predecessor is the syncretistic goddess which is most widely known under the name of Isis" (p. 36).

3. "Wisdom in the New Testament," *Interpreter's Dictionary of the Bible,* p. 958.

4. In the first sermon in *Sermons on the Mount, Harmony of the Gospels, Homilies on the Gospels;* cited by Jennifer Perone Heimmel, *"God Is Our Mother": Julian of Norwich and the Medieval Image of Christian Feminine Divinity* (Ann Arbor: University Microfilms International, 1980), p. 24.

5. In *Questionum Evangelium;* cited by Heimmel, p. 25.

6. Leonard Swidler quotes Raphal Patai's assertion that Wisdom 8:3 depicts Wisdom as God's wife (cf. 8:9). Philo also stated point blank that God is the husband of Sophia (Wisdom). See *Biblical Affirmations of Woman,* pp. 47–48.

7. "Wisdom in the New Testament," p. 958.

8. *The Feminine in Jungian Psychology and in Christian Theology* (Evanston: Northwestern University Press, 1971), pp. 315–316.

9. "The Catholic Concept of the Feminine," *Bucknell Review,* XXIV (Spring 1978), p. 67.

10. "A Few Thoughts on the Individuation Process in Women," *Spring* (New York: The Analytical Psychology Club, 1941), p. 84; cited by Ulanov.

11. On this topic, see Stephanie A. Demetrakoupoulos, "Anais Nin and the Feminine Quest for Consciousness: The Quelling of the Devouring Mother and the Ascension of the Sophia [Wisdom]," *Bucknell Review,* XXIV (Spring 1978), 119–136.

·18·

The Divine Milieu

Although the topic of this book is biblical images of God as female (God as "she"), women have through the ages been so closely associated with the earth and the water and various natural phenomena that it seems important to include such imagery, however briefly.

Mary Daly defines the "eternal masculine stereotype"— a more precise wording than "masculine principle"—as implying "hyper-rationality (in reality, frequently reducible to pseudo-rationality), objectivity, aggressivity, the possession of dominating and manipulative attitudes toward persons and the environment, and the tendency to construct boundaries between the self (and those identified with the self) and 'the Other'."[1] Women have, of course, for centuries been defined as "the Other." So have the nonwhite races. So has the natural environment. It is no accident that the most compelling book concerning nuclear warfare is called *The Fate of the Earth*. In it Jonathan Schell tries to shock us into realizing that our technology has brought us to the point where we may destroy Mother Earth and all her children in one devastating holocaust. Where weaponry is as all-encompassing as nuclear warheads, there *is* no "Other."

Clearly, the language of liturgy, prayer, sermon, and hymnody ought to tend toward dissolving the patriarchal barriers between self and "Other." That will be one of the

effects of utilizing the biblical images of God as female—
and also of God as a natural phenomenon or other "thing."

Genesis 1:28 records a divine charge to the human male
and female that has been widely misunderstood: "Be fruit-
ful, and multiply, and replenish the earth, and subdue it;
and have dominion...." Precisely because those words
were read through lenses colored by the "masculine stereotype," the natural environment has been dominated and
oppressed, manipulated and abused in ways analogous to
the patriarchal use and abuse of women. By lifting up the
biblical images of God as a part of nature, we can perhaps
help ourselves remember that "everything that lives is
holy."[2] Indeed, if we are to believe that imaging God con-
fers holiness, even certain things that *don't* live (in any organic sense) are holy. For instance, Exodus 3:14 says that
God is a verb of being: God tells Moses that God's name is
"I Am Who I Am," and Moses is instructed to tell the children of Israel that "I Am has sent me to you." Jesus also
identified with the verb of being: "I tell you most so-
lemnly," Jesus said, "before Abraham ever was,/ I Am"
(John 8:58). The proper pronoun for a verb is, of course, *it*.

Had humankind not been blinded by sinful notions of
dominance and submission, we would have seen that Genesis 1:28 was conferring the natural environment upon us
as a commonwealth to be respected and cherished. It is
madness to destroy that which sustains us. As any athlete
or gardener can testify, the only way to "subdue" nature is
to "obey" nature. If we defy nature's laws about the way
plants grow, we will have no plants. If we intend to run
faster than anyone else, we must learn the rhythm of our
own bodies in relationship to the track under our feet and
the air we move in. Humankind is holy, but so is the environment. Therefore, respectful mutuality is the proper
relationship between people and nature, people and things.
Natural images for God, lifted up and proclaimed, may

help us get back into harmony with the world we inhabit.

Here are some of the major images of God as an object or natural phenomenon found in the Hebrew and Christian Scriptures. Repeatedly, God is pictured in terms of *water* (traditionally a feminine element): look, for instance, at Psalms 1:3, 46:4; Isaiah 27:3, 6; 41:17–18; 44:3, 4; 55:1; 58:11; Ezekiel 16:9, 36:25; John 3:5, 7:37–39; Ephesians 5:26; and Hebrews 10:22. God is referred to as a *rock* in Deuteronomy 32:4, 15; Psalms 15; 18:2, 31:3, 71:3; I Corinthians 10:4, and elsewhere. In Ephesians 3:17 and Colossians 2:7, God as love, or Christ, is the *ground* in which believers are rooted. God is depicted as *fire* in such passages as Exodus 13:21; Psalm 78:14; Isaiah 4:4, Zechariah 4; Malachi 3:2–3; Acts 2:3; and Hebrews 12:29. And God is pictured as *wind* in I Kings 19:11 (cf. Acts 2:2), Ezekiel 37:9–14, John 3:8, and I Corinthians 12:11. For many centuries people believed that the four basic elements of the universe were earth, air, fire, and water. So the biblical images of God as rock and ground (earth), wind (air), fire, and water encompassed the whole universe and therefore affirmed the holiness of all things.

In addition to depicting God under the more general category of water, the biblical authors used rain and dew as emblems of God in Psalm 68:9, 72:6, 133:3; Isaiah 18:4; Ezekiel 34:26–27, and Hosea 6:3, 10:12, 14:5. God is also associated with oil in Psalm 45:7. God as *healing* oil is implied in Revelation 3:18; as *consecrating* oil in Exodus 29:7, 30:30 and Isaiah 61:1; as *comforting* oil in Isaiah 61:3 and Hebrews 1:9; as *illuminating* oil in Matthew 25:3–4 and I John 2:20,27.

We have already discussed the biblical images of God as hen, pelican, and eagle because those are specifically *female* images. God's Spirit is also depicted as a dove in Matthew 3:16. Because the dove is an adrogynous image, emblematic of the supreme Goddess yet also considered to be phallic,[3] it is an image of God that draws together and unites all the masculine and feminine imagery concerning God.

When we combine the images of God as pelican, hen, eagle, dove, bear, and lamb (John 1:29) and the traditional image of Christ as fish, we have a tremendous warning against abusing animals. Although they were given to us for food, they are not to be used thoughtlessly. Everything that lives is, indeed, holy.

It is instructive to look at the kinds of things Jesus used to describe the realm or kingdom of heaven: ordinary seeds, a field full of wheat corrupted by tares, a tiny mustard seed, three measures of flour, a treasure hidden in a field, the pearl of great price, a large fishing net, and the new and old contents of a house. These are all ordinary things, for the most part lowly things, identified with either earth or water and therefore with the feminine. Yet they are associated by Jesus with the coming of the divine commonwealth!

The biblical images of God as natural phenomena will, if utilized, help us recognize our milieu as divine. If we need further encouragement so to utilize them, perhaps Ephesians 1:10 will help. That passage tells us that it is God's plan to "bring everything together under Christ, as head, / everything in the heavens and everything on earth." As Saint Francis knew long ago, the New Creation makes sisters and brothers out of all the birds, the beasts, the fish, the sun, the moon, the stars, and all of humankind.

NOTES

1. *Beyond God the Father* (Boston: Beacon Press, 1973), p. 15.
2. William Blake, "A Song of Liberty."
3. Ernest Jones, *Essays in Applied Psychoanalysis* (New York: International Universities Press, 1964), Volume 2, pp. 326 and 341.

·19·

Some Suggestions and Conclusions

When all is said and done, the Bible contains *massively* more masculine God-language and male God-imagery than female imagery. People who prefer male supremacy are, of course, delighted by that fact. People with a strong sense of human justice are sometimes repelled by the same fact. In other words, we may all see the same thing, but feel differently about what we see.

My own sense is that it is perfectly natural for the Bible to contain a vast predominance of masculine God-language, springing as it does out of a deeply patriarchal culture. Although I hold a very high view of biblical inspiration, I also understand that the Bible is as dual-dimensional as the nature of Jesus: fully divine and fully human. The biblical authors were socialized in a culture where anything—even a milk-cow—would be raised to special honor by a masculine suffix. After all, males held all the honor and power in society. Nothing would seem more natural to them than to honor God by exclusively masculine references.

And nothing would seem more *un*natural to them than to introduce the female and the feminine into their descriptions of the divine. Yet, as we have seen, they did exactly that! Not very often, of course. But the miracle is that they ever used *any* images of God as female at all.

It's like the old story of the pessimist and the optimist.

Confronted by a glass containing water to the half-way point, the pessimist will describe it as half-empty, the optimist as half-full. Confronted by the relatively few biblical images of God as female, many people will use what I will call the "half-empty theory" of saying that this paucity shows the bankrupt condition of Judeo-Christianity. Irrelevant to women, Judeo-Christianity and its Holy Book must be discarded because women do not find their own stories included there.

Or perhaps the "half-empty theory" may take another form: emphasizing that the few biblical images of God as female represent simply the recurrence of repressed Goddess-worship from the ancient religions replaced by Judeo-Christianity.[1] Although the Goddess had been officially exorcized, the theory goes, Jews and Christians could not entirely wipe out her influence within their spirits. Even Leonard Swidler utilizes this theory: "Lady Wisdom, Hokmah, is also doubtless the Hebrew expression of the ancient Goddess that has been biblically canonized, for the Goddess was widely worshipped as the source of all knowledge and wisdom, particularly in the symbol of the Serpent Goddess.... The highly respected scholar Hans Conzelmann, after careful analysis, concluded similarly: 'Personified Wisdom's ... predecessor is the syncretistic goddess which is most widely known under the name of Isis.' "[2] This theory makes the biblical images of God as female seem like heretical hangovers rather than important insights into the nature of divinity and humanity.

Personally, I prefer the "half-full theory," by which I mean an understanding that God's Spirit circumvented the conscious beliefs of the biblical authors through the use of imagery. Authentic images (metaphors, symbols) arise from the unconscious mind and are therefore less polluted by socialization than the conscious ideas instilled into us by our culture. Therefore people who would never directly call God "She," for fear of insulting God in a male-oriented culture, nevertheless were inspired to use images of God as a mother, a female bird, a housewife, a bakerwoman, and so forth. In fact, because the biblical images of God as female run counter to any of the conscious concepts of males socialized patriarchally, they constitute a very strong argument for the inspired nature of the Hebrew and Christian Scriptures. Ordinarily the group in power does not depict God in terms of the group they are oppressing. But in the case of the Bible, it happened. The fact that it happened *rarely* should not surprise us. The fact that it happened at all *should* surprise us. And delight us. And challenge us.

If, despite patriarchal assumptions, the biblical authors utilized images of God as female, what about ourselves? We have the whole cultural tradition to learn from. We can learn from the mistakes of the twelfth-century Cistercian monks, who freely utilized female God-imagery but rarely, if ever, allowed that to carry over into their treatment of real women. We can learn from the mistake of John Donne, who utilized female God-language yet preached the inferiority of the human female. Not because we are better than they but because we have them to learn from, we do not have to continue making the same mistakes.

A few decades ago in literary circles T.S. Eliot introduced the term "dissociation of sensibility." His meaning of the term need not concern us here, for our focus is on the truly *devastating* dissociation of sensibility that can see literary images as one thing and life as another. If God can be compared to a woman as well as to a man, then no real-flesh human being should be categorically subordinated to another on the basis of her sex. Let me give one more illustration of the problem. In *Paradise Lost*, the great seventeenth-century poet John Milton depicted God the Father and the Son in traditional, exclusively male terminology. But when he dealt with his own Muse, his own inspiring

Spirit, when he related to God *as God was present in his own experience*, he utilized both male and female images.[3] He even depicted himself as stereotypically feminine, a passive receptacle, in relationship to the divine woman:

> . . . my Celestial Patroness . . . deigns
> Her nightly visitation unimplor'd,
> And dictates to me slumb'ring, or inspires
> Easy my unpremeditated Verse (*PL* IX, 21–24).

He admits that he will not be able to do justice to his subject if the argument of it is simply his own, "Not Hers who brings it nightly to my Ear" (*PL* IX, 47).

Yet when it came to real-life treatment of real-life women, Milton did not take a stand for full sexual equality. He was far more feminist than most males of his day[4] (a much more oppressive era than, say, Chaucer's in the fourteenth century), but he was not able to carry his intuitive insight about the divine nature into full social implementation.

We do not have to continue to suffer from such dissociation of sensibility. However, we cannot fully implement human sexual equality as a basis for every other kind of equality until we have first renewed our minds by thinking and speaking only in terms that affirm that equality. What beginnings can the faith-community make toward that full implementation?

We can resolutely learn to speak of God in an all-inclusive way. I like Schubert M. Ogden's definition of God as "The Thou with the greatest conceivable degree of real relatedness to others—namely, relatedness to *all* others." For this reason, God is "the most truly absolute Thou any mind can conceive."[5] This *Thou*, this Absolute Relatedness, may be referred to as *He*, *She*, or *It* because this *Thou* relates to everyone and everything. This *Thou* is violated and enraged when any being is excluded from relationship, subordinated and dehumanized by our lovelessness and our sinful urge toward domination. This *Thou* is a jealous God—not jealous in the sense of one prideful Potentate who insists on having all attention focused on Himself, but jealous instead that He/She/It be recognized everywhere in everyone and everything. Jealous also that we may not separate out some part of the creation and make it our god. Unfortunately, our almost exclusive focus on male God-imagery has resulted in an idolatry of the male. We must take immediate steps to exorcize that idolatry, learning once again to relate to the *Thou* who encompasses and energizes *all* being, *all* becoming.

Our idolatrous thought-patterns could be moved toward healing through judicious changes in the way we read the Bible both in church and at home. If we truly believe that the Bible's intentions are all-inclusive—that redemption is intended for everyone—we will not want to continue practices that exclude certain listeners. Like the apostle Paul, we will want to "make [ourselves] all things to all [people] in order to save some at any cost" (I Corinthians 8:23). Just as we have substituted modern terms so that ordinary people can comprehend the intent of the biblical authors, we can now render the English language inclusively, so that God's universally loving intentions will become clear to all who listen.

Kathryn Ann Piccard has made some suggestions that could help us in this process.[6] Writes Piccard, "Hebrew and Greek use grammatical gender in a different way than English does, and this makes translation challenging. In general, gender pronouns in reference to God should not be translated by English words which suggest a sexual nature for God, such as he, his, etc. Instead the translator can replace the pronoun with the noun it refers to, such as God, God's, Yahweh, etc." Instead of the reflexive "God Himself," we may plausibly substitute "God's Very Self," or (less emphatically) "God's Self."

Piccard rightly points out that "The exception comes in passages where gender pronouns refer to a sex-specific image, whether animal or human. In translating [and reading] these passages it is appropriate to employ English gender pronouns matching the sex of the one imaged. But even in these passages the noun may be used instead of the pronoun referring to it." In other words, in reading Deuteronomy 32:11 about God as Mother Eagle, the lectionary reader might substitute "she" even if the particular translation utilizes "its,"or "his"; and certainly a sermon on the topic might include and empower women and the "feminine component" in men by utilizing *she* concerning God. But it is also possible to avoid pronouns concerning God. In general this avoidance is a good idea, simply because such an overwhelming percentage of those pronouns would have to be masculine.

If our goal is pointed inclusion of females and the feminine in the language of worship, we may find ourselves utilizing female God-images and pronouns as frequently as possible, and utilizing male pronouns only in those contexts where they are absolutely necessary, such as in some of the Father/Son images of the New Testament. A heavily masculine-sounding term like "the Son of Man" may be transformed into "The Human One," a term that effectively communicates the humility and inclusiveness of Jesus' favorite way of referring to himself. Of course, when the National Council of Churches Lectionary Committee has completed its work, and the inclusive-language Lectionary is available, the task of implementing inclusive language in worship services will be considerably eased.

I like Kathryn Ann Piccard's emphasis on using the *full spectrum* of biblical images of God—human, nonhuman, material, and nonmaterial. If we use only material analogies (God as rock, water, and so forth) we are underemphasizing the transcendent nature of God; we need also such nonmaterial images of God as love, word, spirit, verb, or light. If we use only human images of God (male or female) then anthropomorphism can be overdone and chauvinistic abuse of the natural environment can result. If we use role images (God as Father, or Husband, or Mother, for instance) to deify and/or justify sex role stereotypes, then "a sin of sexism occurs." It is all too easy to divert ourselves away from worshipping God to worshipping one particular image of God: and that is idolatry. The best way to heal ourselves of the idolatry we have fallen into is to utilize the full range of biblical imagery for God.

I have already expressed my belief that the Lord's prayer might be addressed to "Our Father/Mother who is in Heaven." Certainly Jesus' own images of God as female assure us that his intention was never to portray God as exclusively masculine; so we know that "Father/Mother" would not violate his understanding of the divine nature. If, however, a congregation cannot bear to alter the traditional wording, surely the prayer could be set in a context where the masculine reference will function inclusively rather than exclusively. For instance, if the lead-in to the recitation of the Lord's prayer utilized a biblical image of God as female, and the first words after the *amen* utilized a biblical image of God as a natural phenomenon or immaterial attitude (like love or hope), then the prayer's reference to father would be effectively inclusive.

As for the doxology, the following form is already in use in some churches:

> Praise God from whom all blessings flow,
> Praise God all creatures here below,
> Praise God above, ye heavenly host:
> Creator, Christ, and Holy Ghost.

Now obviously Creator and Christ are *not* the same as Father and Son. Creator and Christ do not express the interrelationship between the first two "persons" of the divine triad. But since "Holy Ghost" has *never* expressed the inter-relationship between the first two "persons" and the third, and since relationship can never seem inclusive when described only in terms of male to male, this new version is more parallel, more accurate, and more wholistic. God is depicted in three functions or manifestations, each named in parallel fashion, each named in such a way that the inter-relationship could take place in any appropriate form: the Creator's or the Spirit's motherhood or fatherhood of the Christ, the Christ's motherly or fatherly nurturance of the Spirit, the brotherly or sisterly function of the triad, and so forth.

Changing liturgical language, such as the language in *The Book of Common Prayer*, is not going to be easy. Neither is changing the language in our old-standby hymns. But at issue is the health of our relationships to others, to ourselves, and to our God. The effort is worthwhile.

Jennifer Perrone Heimmel's doctoral dissertation on Julian of Norwich contains some insights that may provide us with additional motivation for the long voyage of God-language changes and the social changes that must be implemented in their wake. Julian's *Revelations of Divine Love* demonstrates, first, the wasteful energy Christian women have been forced to expend in order to assure ourselves that Christian faith-language really does include us despite its excluding sound. In Chapter 79 of the Long Text, Julian says that she came to realize that the comfort of the Lord was "for the general man, that is to say every man ... *of which man I am a member.*"[7] If our language is constantly inclusive, such a realization will be natural rather than hard-won.

Furthermore, Dame Julian's quest for self-knowledge is intimately connected with her quest for knowledge of God's nature: "And so," Julian writes, "I saw most surely that it is quicker for us and easier to come to the knowledge

of God than it is to know our own soul. For our soul is so
deeply grounded in God and so endlessly treasured that we
cannot come to knowledge of it until we first have knowledge of God, who is the Creator to whom it is united."[8]
Thus Julian is led to an image of a Christian feminine as
well as masculine God, a God in whom her own soul is
deeply grounded. She discovers that indeed all people and
all things are reflections of that one all-inclusive divinity.
Like the women in *For Colored Girls Who Have Considered Suicide When the Rainbow Is Enuf,* Dame Julian
finds God in her soul and loves Her fiercely.

One other insight: Dame Julian wrote a short version of
her *Revelations of Divine Love* which she then expanded
over a period of twenty years into the Long Text. Not only
does the Long Text contain greatly expanded images of
God as female, but it also shows a marked decrease in dis-
paraging comments about herself. Whereas the short version contains references to herself as a weak, frail woman,
the long version drops these, except for the factual admis-
sion that she was uneducated at the time she received her
visions. Instead there is a new self-respect, as in the statement that "I powerfully, wisely, and deliberately chose
Jesus for my heaven."[9] Furthermore, many of the Short
Text's pronouns for the soul, humanity, and God as "he,"
"his," and "him," are deliberately changed in the Long
Text to "she" "we," "us," "thee," and "these." Clearly as
Dame Julian matured in her understanding that God the
Father is also God the Mother, her own self-concept was
strengthened, quieted, and made secure. For our society, it
is a consummation devoutly to be wished!

The structure of Julian's book and her favored approach
to problems in general is a movement from contrast and contradiction (dualism) toward a transcendent,
reconciling plane. For instance, Chapter 51 "begins with a
striking series of contrasting twos and yet works its way to-

wards a transcending and harmonizing vision of the Trinity. Surely it is no coincidence that after this vivid enactment of harmony overcoming opposition the very next sentence of the book [the first sentence of Chapter 52] contains the first clear statement that God is our mother: 'God rejoices that he is our Mother.' "[10]

Harmony overcoming opposition. How badly our society needs that! How badly our fragmented personalities need that! In a God who transcends and yet contains both female and male, both masculine and feminine, the battle of the sexes can at last be stilled.

NOTES

1. This theory is easy to come by. See, for instance, Raphael Patai, *The Hebrew Goddess* (New York: KTAV Publishing House, 1967; repr. Avon, 1968).

2. *Biblical Affirmations of Woman* (Philadelphia: Westminster Press, 1979), p. 36.

3. See Virginia R. Mollenkott, "Some Implications of Milton's Androgynous Muse," *Bucknell Review*, XXIV (Spring 1978), 27-36).

4. See Virginia R. Mollenkott, "Milton and Women's Liberation," *Milton Quarterly*, VII (Dec. 1973), 99-103.

5. *The Reality of God and Other Essays*, cited by Stephanie A. Demetrakopoulis in "Anais Nin and the Feminine Quest for Consciousness: The Quelling of the Devouring Mother and the Ascension of the Sophia," *Bucknell Review*, XXIV (Spring 1978), p. 133.

6. Informally published worksheets entitled *Bible Images of God*, 1977 (see Chapter Two, endnote 4).

7. Cited by Heimmel, in *"God Is Our Mother": Julian of Norwich and the Medieval Image of Christian Feminine Divinity* (Ann Arbor: University Microfilms, 1980), p. 88. Julian quotations have been modernized in accordance with the translation by Edmund Colledge, O.S.A., and James Walsh, S.J., in the Paulist Press edition of 1978.

8. Chapter 56 of the Long Text, cited by Heimmel, p. 92.

9. Chapter 19 of the Long Text, cited by Heimmel, p. 94.

10. Heimmel, p. 108.